YOUTH AND THE TEMPLE

YOUTH AND THE TEMPLE

WHAT YOU WANT TO KNOW
AND HOW YOU CAN PREPARE

Chad Hawkins

BOOKCRAFT
SALT LAKE CITY, UTAH

Library of Congress Cataloging-in-Publication Data

Hawkins, Chad S., 1971-
   Youth and the temple / Chad S. Hawkins.
     p.   cm.
   Summary: Explores the history and meaning of Mormon temples and suggests how to keep the temple of the body worthy of entering the temple building for ordinances and worship. Includes bibliographical references.
   ISBN 1-57008-846-2 (pbk.)
   1. Mormon temples.   2. Mormon youth—Religious life.   [1. Mormon temples.   2. Conduct of life.   3. Christian life.   4. Mormons.]   I. Title.
   BX8643.T4 H39 2002
   246'.9589332—dc21   2002006671

Printed in the United States of America   54459-6970
Malloy Lithographing Incorporated, Ann Arbor, MI

10   9   8   7   6   5   4   3   2

*Dedicated to my children
as they prepare for the temple*

CONTENTS

INTRODUCTION

I began taking a special interest in temples when I was seventeen years old. It was then that I drew and published my first temple drawing. What started out as a favorite pastime turned into a way to finance my mission and college education, and eventually developed into a career.

Because of the things I have learned, I am grateful for the opportunity to research, visit, and draw the sacred and beautiful temples. It has been especially inspiring to meet and interview faithful members of The Church of Jesus Christ of Latter-day Saints who have participated in the construction and operation of temples. Their devotion has strengthened my testimony of the divinity of temple work. My hope is that the information and stories in this book will help you have, in the words of President Howard W. Hunter, "an increased desire to be worthy of a temple recommend and to attend the temple as frequently as circumstances allow."[1]

Over the years I have spoken at many firesides and youth conferences about our sacred temples. These speaking opportunities began to come along when I was still in high school. I loved to speak to people my age about what I was discovering. Meeting with youth to talk about the temple continues to be one of the joys of my life. I hope this book will expand your understanding of the importance of the temple and give you an even greater desire to be worthy to receive your temple blessings. There is no better shield against the temptations that are so much a part of today's world.

One of my most memorable speaking experiences occurred in 1994 during a Salt Lake City high school seminary devotional. Hoping to make a strong impression and dramatize the importance of being married in the temple, I decided to do something unusual. I had been dating a girl named Stephanie, and at the conclusion of my talk, I invited her to join me at the pulpit. She was a little embarrassed to get up in front of more than five hundred seminary students, but she was a good sport and came forward. With her standing at my side, I told the audience that I was looking forward to being married in the temple and that I wanted to introduce them to the beautiful young woman whom I hoped to marry there. With Stephanie turning a few shades of red, I dropped to one knee and asked her to marry me. The audience was stunned, almost as much as Stephanie, and you can imagine my anxiety as I waited for her answer. I was relieved when she said yes. A "no" would have ruined a lot more than my object lesson.

One of the things that appeals to me about temple work is knowing that I can help my departed ancestors, who were unable to enjoy Church membership while living, to claim their blessings of exaltation. President Gordon B. Hinckley has demonstrated his love and enthusiasm for this work by dedicating or rededicating more than seventy temples.

"We are living in one of the most significant and important epochs in the history of the Church and in the history of God's work among His people," he said in describing this season of unprecedented temple building. "We are living in the greatest era of temple building ever witnessed."[2]

In the year 2000 alone, thirty-four new temples were dedicated—as many as were built in the 108 years between

1877 and 1985! We are witnessing a modern-day miracle and the fulfillment of prophecy. What a wonderful time to be alive. Amazed by what has happened, people frequently tell me that they remember when the Church had fewer than ten temples. Because temples will one day literally dot the earth, we will probably amaze our future children and grandchildren when we tell them that we remember when there were only one hundred temples!

While researching the history of the temples, I was impressed by the faithfulness demonstrated by young people who have been involved in temple work. I have included some of their stories here in the hope that their experiences may inspire you and strengthen your understanding of and love for the temple.

While the Church prepares temples for its members, members must prepare themselves for the temples. Regardless of your age, now is the time to make your plans. In the first part of this book, you'll find information about how you can get involved today in temple worship and work. For example, you can make the temple a part of your life by going to the temple with a youth group to perform baptisms for the dead, by helping your family identify ancestors whose temple work needs to be done, and by participating in temple open houses and dedications.

Part two of this book discusses preparation for receiving temple ordinances. You'll learn some things you can do to be better prepared to make temple covenants. You'll become acquainted with some important new vocabulary. And you'll find answers to questions about temple marriage and other key principles.

In part three, you'll find a quiz that offers a fun way to test your temple knowledge. Take it with your friends. You'll also read excerpts from dedicatory prayers of many of the temples that demonstrate the concern and love our prophets have for the youth of the Church.

Although your first trip to the temple may seem far away, preparing to go to the temple now can be a part of your everyday life. In looking forward to that day, you need to remember that your body is also a temple. I promise you that if you will keep yourself clean and pure, one of the happiest experiences you will ever have will be to kneel at an altar in the temple and be sealed to your eternal companion. So prepare now to "make the temple, with temple worship and temple covenants and temple marriage, [your] ultimate earthly goal and the supreme mortal experience."[3]

NOTES

1. Howard W. Hunter, "Follow the Son of God," *Ensign*, November 1994, 88.
2. Gordon B. Hinckley, "Rejoice in This Great Era of Temple Building," *Ensign*, November 1985, 54.
3. Hunter, 88.

PART ONE

WHAT IS A TEMPLE?

A temple is more than a church or chapel and more than the grandest synagogue or cathedral. It is a house of the Lord. "A temple is literally a house of the Lord, a holy sanctuary in which sacred ceremonies and ordinances of the gospel are performed by and for the living and also in behalf of the dead. A place where the Lord may come, it is the most holy of any place of worship on the earth."[1] As you will learn, the ordinances performed in the temple are the most sacred ever revealed and are essential for exaltation.

Before latter-day temples are dedicated, they are merely beautiful buildings, featuring the highest quality craftsmanship, decor, and furnishings. But it is not the chandeliers, gold leafing, stained glass, or artwork that make a temple unique and sacred. It is the exercising of priesthood keys and authority to perform sacred ordinances that makes a temple the house of the Lord, the most holy place of worship on earth. Once dedicated by authority from God, these beautiful edifices become holy sanctuaries. If you have been to a temple open house or performed baptisms for the dead, you know the feeling of reverence and beauty found in the temple.

The Kirtland Temple was the first temple built in the latter days, but it was certainly not the first temple built by the Lord's people. Since the time of Adam, faithful followers of Jesus Christ have been commanded to build temples. The

7

Israelites had a portable tabernacle, which served as a temple while the people traveled in the wilderness. King Solomon and King Herod each built temples in Jerusalem. Nephi constructed a temple, patterned after the temple of Solomon, on the American continent (2 Nephi 5:16). The Book of Mormon also mentions a temple in Zarahemla (Mosiah 1:18). Much later, the resurrected Lord appeared to the Nephites as they were gathered around the temple in the land of Bountiful (3 Nephi 11:1–10). In times of extreme poverty or emergency, temple ordinances have been performed on mountaintops or in other wilderness areas.[2]

During the dark centuries of the Apostasy, the Lord's temples ceased to exist. Not until the restoration of the gospel in the nineteenth century were the powers and blessings of the

temple manifest again on earth. The First Vision in 1820 set in motion the reestablishment of the Lord's kingdom and authority among mankind. Shortly after the Church was organized, the Lord commanded the Saints to build a holy house in which he could endow his chosen servants with power (D&C 95:8). Amidst extreme poverty and mounting persecution, the Saints made great sacrifices to build the Kirtland Temple, which the Prophet Joseph Smith dedicated on March 27, 1836.

In the early history of the Church, the Saints began planning temples even before building their homes. Wherever they settled, their first concern and efforts went toward building a temple. The gospel plan the Lord has revealed is not complete without a temple because only in the temple are necessary ordinances for the plan of salvation administered.

During construction of the Nauvoo Temple, the Prophet Joseph Smith said, "The Church is not fully organized, in its proper order, and cannot be, until the Temple is completed."[3]

Temple worship is one of the marks of the true Church in any dispensation.[4] You and I are fortunate to be living at a time when the number of temples has multiplied unbelievably. According to prophecy, hundreds of temples will eventually dot the earth.[5]

Only in the temple are Heavenly Father's crowning blessings of life given to his children. Only in the temple can the fullness of the priesthood be realized. The essence of all we do in the Church centers on the temple. The temple serves as a setting where we can focus on our most ennobling thoughts and feelings. Within the temple we may feel closer to our Heavenly Father than in any other place on earth. At the temple's altars we kneel before God and enter into covenants that will bless our lives both here on earth and in eternity. Temples are powerful reminders of the love our Eternal Father has for us; they provide the ordinances we are required to receive if we desire to return to his presence.

I hope you'll stay with me on this voyage of discovery as we explore together many important things about the house of the Lord and what you can anticipate as you prepare for your own temple ordinances.

NOTES

1. Bible Dictionary, s.v. "Temple."
2. Bible Dictionary, s.v. "Temple."
3. Smith, *History of the Church*, 4:603.
4. Bible Dictionary, s.v. "Temple."
5. Young, *Discourses of Brigham Young*, 395.

YOUTH WHO HAVE PARTICIPATED IN TEMPLE BUILDING

Throughout history, the Lord has tried his chosen people by requiring them to make significant sacrifices. More than 150 years ago, for example, the Lord called upon the Saints to sacrifice their time, talents, possessions, and other resources to ensure that beautiful temples were built in Kirtland and Nauvoo. Sacrifice has always been synonymous with building temples.

In the spring of 1999, while I was preparing to sketch the St. George Temple, I asked the temple engineer if he would allow me to take some reference photographs from the roof of the nearby visitors center. He was kind enough to meet me at 4 A.M. and spend time with me on the roof. As we waited for the sun to rise he said, "The sun won't come up for another hour; would you like a tour of the temple?" I held a current temple recommend (we'll discuss temple recommends in chapter five), so I readily accepted the opportunity.

With no one else in the building, he escorted me through places visitors don't normally see. While we were in the audiovisual room, he pointed out the original red sandstone walls. He then reached up and snapped off a small piece of mortar. Although it was more than one hundred years old, the mortar did not crumble. He showed me how it had been strengthened by human hair added to the mix.

As he held the mortar reverently in his hands, he asked,

"Chad, what kind of testimony do you think this sister had when she donated her hair to the temple?"

As I pondered his question he added, "I want you to always remember that when the Saints were asked to donate everything they had to the temple, they literally donated everything they had."

I will never forget the spiritual insight I received at that moment. Suddenly that unnamed woman and what she had contributed became very real. Contemplating her sacrifice reminded me that temples are special places and that we should never take them for granted.

In my study of temples, I have discovered many such stories. I have been particularly inspired by how young Latter-day Saints have been involved in the construction of temples.

In Nauvoo, for instance, young people carried water and

food to the workmen, and they helped their mothers make clothing for temple laborers. When the Logan Utah Temple was being built, young people gathered clothing and old rags, ripping them into strips and then organizing them by colors so their mothers could use the material to create carpet for the temple.

Many such well-known and inspiring stories of sacrifice and inspiration are associated with the construction of earlier temples, but similar stories of sacrifice, hard work, and faith can be told about the temples being built today. I hope the following examples will inspire you, strengthen your testimony, and help you appreciate more fully the temples that you attend.

LOGAN UTAH TEMPLE

Of the $600,000 contributed toward financing the construction of the Logan Utah Temple, $2,300 came from children in the Cache Valley Stake who contributed to a Sunday School "nickel fund." One curious young boy who had contributed to this fund visited the temple during its construction. While attempting to examine the temple by climbing its scaffolding, he was stopped by a guard, who asked him what he was doing. The boy said he had paid his nickel to the temple nickel fund and "therefore felt he had a right to see it."[1]

As the Saints willingly sacrificed time and money to build the temple, God's power was witnessed in the preservation of many lives, including that of a nineteen-year-old Brother James, who was returning to Logan with a large wagonload of lumber for the temple.

"All went well for a short distance, until the wagon wheel

hit a soft spot. The riverbank caved in, dropping the two wheels and throwing Brother James on the bottom of the stream, with his big load upside down on top of him. It took the workmen nearly half an hour to break the binding and to roll the wagon and lumber from the river. Brother James had been under water for this full length of time. They laid his body on the bank, covered it with a blanket and told one of the boys to get on a horse and come to Logan to tell the parents what had happened to their son.

"Before the horse could be bridled, the blanket began to move and Brother James was up on his feet. Evidently his wind had been knocked out as his load went over, and he had not breathed for thirty minutes, and had no water in his lungs. The ice-cold water had slowed his body processes, and he had no brain or bodily damage of any kind. He was none the worse for the experience, and reloaded his wagon and brought it on down to the temple."[2]

The following year, the young man was called on a mission to England.

MANTI UTAH TEMPLE

As members were called upon to make contributions to build the Manti Utah Temple, most donated such things as beef, chicken, wheat, flour, and clothing. Following the wheat harvest, children would search the fields for any remaining wheat. They would then give this gleaned wheat to their mothers, who used it to make bread for temple workmen.[3]

SALT LAKE TEMPLE

Nearly three weeks of dedicatory services followed the completion of the Salt Lake Temple, allowing nearly seventy thousand members to participate. On April 21 and 23, 1893, special dedicatory sessions were held for Sunday School children under eight years of age. About twelve thousand children and their teachers attended these sessions. One sister present at these special sessions wrote, "The Sunday School passing through the Temple and joining in the 'hosannahs' must have been a sight for angels to gaze upon, and undoubtedly myriads of them were present."[4]

LOS ANGELES CALIFORNIA TEMPLE

In February 1952, President David O. McKay encouraged Latter-day Saints in Southern California to shoulder part of the cost of building a temple there. Meeting with twelve hundred ward and stake leaders, he challenged them to raise one million dollars. He then encouraged them to have the "young people, even the children in the 'cradle roll,' contribute to the temple fund, for this is their temple, where they will be led by pure love to take their marriage vows."

The Saints responded with enthusiasm and generous pledges. When a bishop received a $150 pledge from a deacon, he thought that the young man had incorrectly positioned the decimal point. But for two years the boy saved money from his paper route and from mowing lawns. Young women helped beautify the temple's landscaping by contributing roses for a garden. Within three months after the call for donations and pledges, the Saints had far surpassed their goal, raising more than $1.6 million.[5]

JORDAN RIVER UTAH TEMPLE

The Jordan River Utah Temple, unlike other temples built up to that point, was funded entirely by contributions from members living in the area. Challenged by President Spencer W. Kimball to raise needed funds, the Saints undertook a large fund-raising campaign in all 122 stakes of the Salt Lake and Jordan River Utah temple districts. When the fund-raising ended a year later, members had contributed $14.5 million, 10 percent more than their original goal.

This vast amount of money came from the sacrifice of thousands of members. Two young brothers, one eight years old and the other nearly ten, were excited to do their part. They walked door to door, asking neighbors if they would like to buy homemade bread. Soon they had requests for sixteen loaves. They hurried home and told their unsuspecting mother that they needed her to bake sixteen loaves of bread right away. She agreed to join her sons' fund-raising venture, and before long the boys delivered sixteen hot loaves of bread. In all, they sold about thirty loaves for the temple fund. [6]

SYDNEY AUSTRALIA TEMPLE

Soon after the Sydney Australia Temple was announced, regional representatives in the area organized a fund-raising project among the Australian Saints. The members enthusiastically responded to the task, reaching their goal of nearly one million dollars in just six months.

One contribution came as the result of an institute teacher's object lesson. He pretended to have received a letter from the stake president calling on his class to raise eight thousand dollars for the temple. The teacher, wanting to see how his students would react to a difficult challenge, did not actually expect them to raise the money. But after he admitted that the letter was a joke, the class eagerly took on the challenge, deciding that each of the forty students would need to raise two hundred dollars to meet the goal. These young men and women found ways to earn the money, and by the end of the semester they had earned forty dollars more than their goal.

"We had the greatest experience a class could ever wish

for," said John Gibson, the institute teacher. "Our love for each other grew greatly. Our testimonies [of] sacrifice and [of] the Savior also grew."[7]

SAN DIEGO CALIFORNIA TEMPLE

The San Diego California Temple, like other temples, is surrounded by beautiful landscaping and gardens that help create a reverent and appropriate setting for the house of the Lord. As plans were being made for the temple's construction and surrounding grounds, many members, including children, sought ways to contribute their time and talents. Youngsters from 180 different wards and branches in the temple district were given the responsibility of watering and caring for some of the flowers to be used during the temple's dedication. After

San Diego

the dedication, the potted flowers were planted in beds around the flagpole.

Children in northern Mexico also wanted to participate but had to do something different because government restrictions would not allow them to bring plants across the border. They decided to design and make a handcrafted rug for members of the First Presidency to stand on as they laid the temple's cornerstone. A microfiche with the names of all the Primary children in the temple district was later placed in the cornerstone, along with other significant items.[8]

MT. TIMPANOGOS UTAH TEMPLE

Thousands of young people living in forty-three stakes volunteered in many ways to the Mt. Timpanogos Utah Temple. With little notice, thousands showed up to help clean up construction debris around the temple and help with the

Mount Timpanogos

landscaping. During the temple's open house, this army of youth sang in choirs, directed traffic, assisted those in wheelchairs, and opened doors for hundreds of thousands of temple visitors.[9]

Two young women and their mother were given the responsibility of assembling the crystal sconces and the large chandelier in the bride's room. As they began unpacking the chandelier pieces, they could not find the assembly instructions. After realizing the instructions had been discarded, they proceeded with their difficult task, referring only to an eight-by-ten picture of the completed chandelier. With great care, the young women unpacked the many chandelier pieces, which quickly began looking like an intricate puzzle. Feeling overwhelmed, they sought help through prayer.

"We just asked for help in seeing where things should go . . . ," said one of the young women. "We would find one piece. . . . Then we would find another that fit with it. Some of the pieces had to be put in first, or you couldn't get the ones that followed in. We found you could not do them out of order." The process of receiving the inspiration they needed was "just amazing. It showed us that the Lord had his hand even in simple things."

In retrospect, they said putting the chandelier together compared to putting their lives together. They realized that they must order their lives in such a way that their conduct would lead them to the temple. Just as the chandelier required orderly assembly, worthiness for a temple marriage requires orderly preparation: baptism, meeting attendance, service, moral cleanliness, proper dating standards, and righteous living.[10]

SPOKANE WASHINGTON TEMPLE

On May 22, 1999, approximately forty Aaronic Priesthood young men from Spokane's East Stake were given a wonderful honor and responsibility. All of the young men

participated in uncrating the temple's baptistry oxen and carrying them to their permanent position within the temple. Some of the smaller young men were able to maneuver between the oxen and the font and securely bolt the oxen into place.[11]

REGINA SASKATCHEWAN TEMPLE

The two-toned granite that adorns the exterior of the Regina Saskatchewan Temple came from a quarry in Quebec. When it was being placed on the temple, many young people experienced a unique opportunity that they will never forget. After a stake youth conference, the young men and young women gathered at the park across from the temple. Having received permission from Church officials and the temple contractor, they signed their names and the date on the back of the granite pieces that were to be placed on the temple. Construction missionary Sterling L. Burch assisted them and told them exactly where each stone was going to be placed. They walked away knowing that their names were going to become a permanent part of the temple.[12]

Elder Burch initiated another project involving the young men and young women. They were allowed to record on paper their testimonies and commitments to temple worthiness. These treasured documents were then placed in a capsule crafted by Elder Burch. He then selected a young man and a young woman to help place the capsule in the temple's spire, directly beneath the statue of the angel Moroni.

"Right after the angel Moroni was placed into position, I took two of the youth up the scaffolding and had them fasten the capsule right under [Moroni's] feet. I could have easily done this, but I thought, *No, this is for the youth; I want them to do it.* All of the stone was not yet attached to the spire, so all of the youth could look up and see where the box containing their precious feelings, goals, and commitments was permanently placed."

This choice experience serves as a constant reminder to those young people to be true to the testimonies and commitments that are a part of the temple.[13]

RALEIGH NORTH CAROLINA TEMPLE

As with other temples, volunteerism was a hallmark of construction on the Raleigh North Carolina Temple. For example, early on January 23, 1999, about twelve hundred young Latter-day Saints began arriving at the building site to clear out underbrush and small trees to render the site suitable

Raleigh

for a groundbreaking ceremony. The young men and young women worked hard but enjoyed serving the Lord. Although heavy rain had been predicted to fall throughout the day, a temple construction missionary noted that not until five minutes after the last group prepared to leave did it begin to rain.[14]

LOUISVILLE KENTUCKY TEMPLE

Young women from local stakes had a memorable experience hanging crystals on the chandeliers of the Louisville Kentucky Temple. Working in shifts, the young women were awed by what they were doing. As they assembled the chandeliers, they joined in singing songs about the temple.

"They had very beautiful high soprano voices, and it made you think there were groups of angels singing in the temple," said Sister Karla Packer Prestridge, a temple construction

Louisville

missionary. When the chandelier was raised into its permanent position in the celestial room, "many of the girls said, 'When I get married in this temple, I can come and say that I helped with the crystals on that chandelier.'"[15]

BATON ROUGE LOUISIANA TEMPLE

When the marble veneer for the exterior walls of the Baton Rouge Louisiana Temple was shipped to the construction site from Vermont, one of the eighteen-wheel delivery trucks arrived after the construction crew had left. Only the foreman, Max Quayle, was still on the site to receive the shipment of ten crates of marble, each weighing three-quarters of a ton. Brother Quayle unloaded two crates with a forklift, but then a hydraulic line on the forklift broke.

The truck driver needed to quickly get back on the road,

so the only solution seemed to be to unload the truck by hand. A few phone calls and fifteen minutes later, twenty-five young Latter-day Saints arrived ready to assist with the seemingly insurmountable task. They unloaded the remaining eight crates—approximately fifteen thousand pounds of marble. The young men went the extra mile by placing the marble, piece by piece, around the temple, where workers could use it as needed. Then they freed the truck, which was stuck on a pile of sand.[16]

It was a night of hard labor, but the work made the Baton Rouge Louisiana Temple even more precious in the eyes of the young men who participated. The marble story—their contribution to building the temple—will be one they share with their children in years to come.

You may not have the opportunity to assist in the actual construction of a temple or to participate in its open house, but you can still show faith, determination, and gratitude. Become worthy to hold a temple recommend, and promise yourself that you will remain worthy. Participate in baptisms for the dead as often as you can. Prepare for the day you will receive your endowment and be married in the temple. Then give a lifetime of ongoing temple service.

NOTES

1. Cowan, *Temples to Dot the Earth*, 86.
2. Olsen, *Logan Temple*, 73.
3. Cowan, 93.
4. Holzapfel, *Every Stone a Sermon*, 78.
5. Lundwall, *Temples of the Most High*, 206.
6. McKay, *For His House*, 10.
7. "Joke Backfires; Class Donates $8,040," *Church News*, 2 May 1981, 7.

8. "Children Learn about Temple, While Adding to Beauty of Grounds," *Church News*, 8 May 1993, 7.

9. Janet Thomas, "At Home in His House," *New Era*, March 1997, 20.

10. Thomas, 22.

11. *Spokane Temple News*, June 1999, 1.

12. Sterling L. Burch and Joy S. Burch, interview by author, tape recording, 17 September 2000, Regina, Saskatchewan.

13. Burch.

14. Alaire Johnson, "Temple Project History," 1–2 (unpublished).

15. Karla Packer Prestridge and Marvin John Prestridge, interview by author, tape recording, 11 March 2000, Louisville, Kentucky.

16. Weldon Smith and Doris Smith, interview by author, tape recording, 12 September 2000, Baton Rouge, Louisiana.

3
TEMPLE WORTHINESS

Prominently featured on the exterior of all latter-day temples are the words "Holiness to the Lord, the House of the Lord." These words remind all who approach the temple that they must be worthy to enter therein. "Holiness to the Lord" is even engraved on the doorknob of the Salt Lake Temple, reminding those who reach for the temple's door that they must have clean hands and a pure heart.

Because of the sacred nature of temple ordinances, the Lord has set a standard of worthiness for those seeking to

enter his house. This standard prevents those who might not fully understand temple ordinances or who might even treat them disrespectfully from having access to the temple. Because the temple is closed to all but faithful members of the Church, it is tempting to think of what goes on inside as mysterious and secret. But it is more accurate to think of temple work as beautiful and sacred. There is a big difference between reverencing the sacred and keeping a secret.

The first temple constructed in this dispensation was the Kirtland Temple. On April 3, 1836, a week following the temple's dedication, the Lord Jesus Christ appeared within the temple to Joseph Smith and Oliver Cowdery. The Lord accepted the temple and promised to manifest himself therein "if my people will keep my commandments, and do not pollute this holy house" (D&C 110:8). Thus, from the very beginning, members of the restored Church have clearly understood that we enter the temple by invitation, and that gaining admission is a privilege and not a right that automatically comes with Church membership. Only the worthy and spiritually prepared are permitted to enter the Lord's house.

On occasion, the Lord has protected temples from desecration and abuse by those who would harm them or enter them unworthily. One example of such protection occurred at the dedication of the Logan Utah Temple in May 1884. As President John Taylor was watching large numbers of people enter the temple, he suddenly turned to Charles O. Card, superintendent of construction, and said that a certain woman coming through the doorway was not worthy to enter the temple. Brother Card asked her to leave after discovering that she was not even a Latter-day Saint. He found out later that she had purchased a temple recommend from a Church

member. President Taylor had never seen this woman before, but the Spirit had whispered that of all the people in attendance, she was not worthy to be there.[1]

Just as no unclean person should enter the house of the Lord, no unclean thing should enter or defile our bodies. The spirit of the Lord, King Benjamin told his people, "dwelleth not in unholy temples" (Mosiah 2:37). Recognizing the many destructive forces in the world, Church leaders have given us inspired counsel on how we can protect ourselves from worldly evils. Here are some things you can do right now to prepare to receive your temple blessings.

1. Respect your body

When we were born, our eternal spirit was clothed in a mortal body, one of the greatest gifts God has given us. As part of our earthly test, we must learn to control the emotions, appetites, and passions that are part of our physical makeup.

To emphasize the sacredness of the human body, the Lord calls it a temple. "Know ye not that ye are the temple of God, and that the Spirit of God dwelleth in you? If any man defile the temple of God, him shall God destroy; for the temple of God is holy, which temple ye are" (1 Corinthians 3:16–17).

It is not uncommon for some youth to behave recklessly, thinking that their lives and bodies are their own to do with as they please. As a result, they may feel a sense of invincibility, ignoring the counsel of parents and Church leaders in their quest for "fun." But the scriptures teach that "ye are not your own . . . for ye are bought with a price," which is the blood of Christ (1 Corinthians 6:19–21). Our Heavenly Father has given us the freedom to choose how we will act, but he will hold us accountable for what we do with our bodies.

One of the disturbing things about modern life is the graffiti that blights our cities and towns. We see graffiti messages, many of them hate-filled, scrawled on buildings, bridges, overpasses, street signs, and fences. To me, this "artwork" is ugly and repulsive, not just because it defaces property but also because it shows disrespect.

Picture your favorite temple and try to imagine how you would feel if its beautiful walls were vandalized by graffiti. That's an awful thought, isn't it? But even more repugnant is the practice of vandalizing the human body with the graffiti of tattoos.

In a talk given to youth and young single adults on November 12, 2000, and broadcast by satellite throughout the Church, President Gordon B. Hinckley gave this warning: "I promise you that the time will come, if you have tattoos, that you will regret your actions. They cannot be washed off. They are permanent. Only by an expensive and painful process can they be removed. If you are tattooed, then probably for the remainder of your life you will carry it with you. I believe the time will come when it will be an embarrassment to you. Avoid it. We, as your Brethren who love you, plead with you not to become so disrespectful of the body which the Lord has given you."[2]

In the same talk, President Hinckley also spoke out against body piercing, which indicates defiance and a lack of self-respect and reverence for the temple that is our body.

You may be tempted to think that getting a tattoo is no big deal, especially if it is small or artistic or placed where it will normally be covered by clothing. But it is a big deal. Your body was created in the image of God. If you deface it by getting a tattoo or mutilating it in any other way, you desecrate the precious temple our Father in Heaven has given you. Conversely, by taking good care of your body, you honor your Creator.

2. Stay morally clean

Because we live in a world saturated with sexuality, one of the greatest temptations we face is the misuse of our sacred powers of procreation. Movies, television shows, popular songs, and even advertisements send the message that it is okay for young people to give free expression to their passions and desires. Sexual morality is portrayed as being outdated and irrelevant, and anyone who values virtue and modesty is made fun of and mocked.

In today's world, even motherhood is considered less significant than having a career and pursuing a life free of family responsibilities. Media messages are slick, enticing, and convincing, and some LDS youth are confused and tempted to ignore or compromise the standards they have been taught.

But indulging in self-gratification results in sorrow and the destruction of families, for "wickedness never was happiness" (Alma 41:10).

Do not be deceived. The powers of procreation are sacred. They are not given to us for recreational purposes, and those who choose to behave immorally put themselves at great risk—both physically and spiritually.

Much of the happiness that will come to you in this life will result from bridling your passions. Physical intimacy between a man and a woman can be rewarding and beautiful when it is shared within a marriage approved of by God. But intimacy is shamefully wrong—like unto murder—when misused outside the covenant of marriage (Alma 39:3–5).

Think about the young couples in your ward that have been married in the temple and then had their first baby. You've seen the loving and grateful way they look at each other and at their newborn. You can have the same experience—if you keep yourself clean and virtuous. Through the righteous exercise of your sacred procreative powers, you can invite into your home little boys and girls who will be your very own, created in your image. Is it any wonder the Lord has directed the building of temples where marriages can be solemnized for all eternity?

President Ezra Taft Benson suggested the following steps to avoid sexual transgression: "Decide now to be chaste. Control your thoughts. Always pray for the power to resist temptation. . . . For those who are single and dating . . . , carefully plan positive and constructive activities so that you are not left to yourselves with nothing to do but share physical affection."[3]

Treat your dates with respect, and expect your dates to

show you the same courtesy. Avoid dating those who would encourage you to compromise your standards by defiling your body or who would offer you the opportunity to defile their body. If you are engaged and planning a temple wedding, make sure you don't use your engagement as an excuse to let down your guard. Don't do anything that would make you ineligible for a temple recommend or cause you to misrepresent your worthiness to your bishop or stake president. Look forward to the joy you will experience as you take your chosen loved one by the hand and enter the temple, knowing that both of you are clean and worthy to be there.

3. Watch your language

As you communicate, your words and tone of voice reveal much about your commitment to the gospel. What you say and how you say it also defines your character. Elder Robert K. Dellenbach said, "The words you use and the way you speak are like a blueprint of who you are deep inside."[4]

Consider the past few days of your life and spend a minute taking an inventory of your language habits by honestly answering the following questions:

- Have I told any dirty or degrading jokes?
- Have I spread gossip?
- Have I raised my voice in an unkind way?
- Have I irreverently used the name of God or Jesus Christ?
- Have I uttered any profane or vulgar words?
- Have I spoken unkindly about others?

Do you need to make some improvements? Are you entirely happy with the impression your language leaves on others? Would you be embarrassed had your parents or bishop been able to hear everything you've said during the past few days?

Sometimes we fall into bad habits that need to be broken. We can begin to break the habit of bad language by staying away from people who use bad language. And we can begin substituting good words for the bad words that come into our minds.

Elder Dellenbach reminded us that because we use our mouth to pray, bear testimony, and bless the sacrament, we should keep it clean. "Our words describe our thoughts and who we really are. As members of the Lord's Church, let us always be aware that the Lord and others are listening."[5]

Avoiding profanity in all its forms is another way we can keep our temple clean and pure.

4. Listen to uplifting music

I have always loved listening to music, but I am thankful my taste in music has matured. What I enjoy listening to today is not what I enjoyed listening to during my high school years. Although I sensed then that the music I liked was often inappropriate, I always found ways to justify my musical taste.

When I began taking an interest in drawing temples, a sister-in-law encouraged me to listen to more appropriate music while making my sketches. Not long afterward, I concluded that if I should not listen to inappropriate music while drawing temples, I should not listen to it at all. This decision meant changing my listening habits and getting rid of most of my music collection. It was the right thing to do. With that negative influence out of my life, I was better prepared to go to the temple before serving my mission.

So much of today's popular music is degrading. If you're honest with yourself, you'll admit that the lyrics offend the

Spirit and are often vulgar and suggestive. If you're serious about resisting temptation, you need to avoid listening to music that ridicules decency and promotes evil. The music you listen to, for better or worse, becomes a part of you. Therefore, surround your personal temple with the protective barrier of good music.

When you repeat to yourself the lyrics from such uplifting hymns as "I Am a Child of God" and hum its soothing melody in your mind, unworthy thoughts and feelings slip away. Because virtue and cleanliness cannot coexist with evil, listening to positive music is a powerful way to invite the Spirit into our lives.

5. Choose good entertainment

It's easy to know when we're keeping the law of tithing and whether we're observing the Word of Wisdom, but selecting appropriate books and magazines, movies, and video games can sometimes be difficult. When considering what to read, watch, or play, we have an excellent guideline in the thirteenth Article of Faith: "If there is anything virtuous, lovely, or of good report or praiseworthy, we seek after these things." We also have this suggestion from the *For the Strength of Youth* pamphlet: "Do not attend, view, or participate in entertainment that is vulgar, immoral, violent, or pornographic in any way."[6] Let those standards be your guide when it comes to choosing entertainment.

Just as tainted food adversely affects the body, unworthy entertainment pollutes the mind and damages the body. Addressing the youth and single adults of the Church, President Gordon B. Hinckley gave this prophetic counsel: "We live in a world that is filled with filth and sleaze, a world that reeks of evil. It is all around us. It is on the television screen. It is at the movies. It is in the popular literature. It is on the Internet. You can't afford to watch it, my dear friends. You cannot afford to let that filthy poison touch you. Stay away from it. Avoid it. You can't rent videos and watch them as they portray degrading things. You young men who hold the priesthood of God cannot mix this filth with the holy priesthood."[7]

The Internet with its limitless resources is a useful and exciting tool. It offers information at the push of a button on virtually any topic. Research that once took hours in a library can now be done in an instant in your home. But like many other tools, the Internet can be dangerous if misused. The *New Era* has offered the following practical guidelines for Internet safety:

- Balance time spent surfing the net with other, more important activities.
- Use the Internet only when parents or other family members are present.
- Use the Internet wisely so you can earn your parents' trust.
- Place the family computer in a common area of the house frequented by family members.
- Set time limits for Internet usage, especially when you're using it for entertainment instead of education.
- Avoid chat rooms. If you find yourself in a chat room, never reveal information about yourself. "If someone asks you for personal information, like your real name, address, phone number, or your parents' credit card number, leave the site immediately. Tell your parents what has happened."[8]

We have been encouraged to nurture our minds by reading "out of the best books" (D&C 109:7). We should apply the same counsel to the kinds of magazines we read. Obviously, publications that contain pornographic images or messages should be avoided at all costs, but we must be careful even with today's mainstream magazines, many of which glamorize sex and violence.

Finding appropriate movies can be a challenge. Many movies tell the story of a great person or historical event, and they may be well made and entertaining, but they may still contain inappropriate scenes. Here are a few tips to guide you in making wise judgments concerning movie selection:

- Check the ratings. Although the ratings are not completely reliable, they offer a place a start. President Ezra Taft Benson counseled, "Don't see R-rated movies or vulgar videos or participate in any entertainment that is immoral, suggestive, or pornographic."[9]
- Read newspaper reviews. Find a movie reviewer you can trust.
- Ask for recommendations from someone who shares your values.

Although I love to curl up with a bowl of popcorn and watch a video, I dread going to the video store to rent them. The corrupt images on many video covers have always offended me, but I've learned to avoid this problem as much as possible by knowing in advance which movie I want to rent. This enables me to go directly to the video and then to the checkout counter, avoiding most of the inappropriate images I would see if I were just wandering around the store.

If you've tried your best to make wise choices, but the

movie you've selected is not up to your standards, turn it off. If you're at a movie theater, walk out. Make up your mind that even though you've spent money, you'd rather turn off a movie than watch something you shouldn't. The only reliable standards are the ones we set for ourselves. From an eternal perspective, movies and television programs that weaken us spiritually are potentially just as harmful as substances that damage us physically. The "just say no" approach works just as well for resisting degrading movies and television programs as it does for avoiding dangerous drugs.

Everything we've said about the negative influence of vulgar music and movies can be applied to violent video games. The most popular of these glorify violence, devalue human life, and promote indifference to suffering. Although seen by the world as harmless fun, these games can dull the senses, strip us of our natural affection, and make us less compassionate. Such evil influence is compatible with the plan of Satan, who is the "father of contention" (3 Nephi 11:29). As peaceable followers of Jesus Christ, we need to elevate our standards and avoid violent entertainment and the raw passions it stimulates.

As you seek out the virtuous, lovely, and praiseworthy, the sensitive whisperings of the Spirit will direct you to choose wisely. Moroni tells us that "the Spirit of Christ is given to every man, that he may know good from evil; wherefore, I show unto you the way to judge; for every thing which inviteth to do good, and to persuade to believe in Christ, is sent forth by the power and gift of Christ" (Moroni 7:16).

We live in the world, but we are capable of resisting the world's evil influences. I was reminded of this truth while researching the history of the Las Vegas Nevada Temple. I had

LAS VEGAS TEMPLE
THE CHURCH OF JESUS CHRIST OF LATTER-DAY SAINTS

the privilege of interviewing the temple's architect, George Tate, who later served as a stake president, stake patriarch, and temple sealer. He pointed out the exceptional quality built into every detail of the temple and showed me a symbol that was unique to the Las Vegas Nevada Temple—the image of a stylized desert lily, which is found on all six spires and in various locations within the temple. Brother Tate explained why he found that flower a particularly appropriate symbol of what the temple represents:

"When our children were small, we used to explore the desert. One thing I remember noticing is that in the valleys along the sides of the roads there were dark green leafy plants with a large white lily flower. I was impressed that even in such an arid climate, the plant was able to produce such a beautiful blossom. We used the desert lily on the temple because just as the beautiful lily stood out amidst the barren desert, the temple stands out in great contrast from the world."[10]

Just as the desert lily and the temple stand out against their contrasting environments, we should likewise stand out by living gospel principles. When you choose to avoid inappropriate entertainment, you are protecting your bodily temple from worldly evils.

6. Live the Word of Wisdom

If you hope to one day enter the sacred temple of the Lord, you must keep your personal temple pure. That means living the Word of Wisdom. Regarding the Lord's law of health, President Ezra Taft Benson counseled, "The Word of Wisdom leads to clean habits, thoughts, and actions. It will make you more receptive to the Spirit of God, which 'cannot dwell in an unclean tabernacle' [Helaman 4:24]. Follow the gospel plan. It provides for solid work, clean entertainment, and activity to promote growth of stature."[11]

Keeping the Word of Wisdom results in both spiritual and physical health (D&C 89:18–21). By abstaining from alcohol, tobacco, coffee, and harmful drugs, you learn to be obedient. If you have friends or family members who are enslaved by physical addictions, you know that they find it difficult to focus on anything except feeding their appetites. They have no time, energy, or inclination to live a Christlike life. That is because dependency on these harmful substances offends the Spirit, making it nearly impossible to feel or hear its promptings. Fortunately, addictions can be overcome.

As plans were being made to construct the Jordan River Utah Temple, Church members living in the temple district were given the opportunity to contribute to the cost of the building. One woman planned to donate funds while still struggling to overcome her dependency on tobacco. Accompanied by her daughter, she told her bishop in an interview that although she didn't have much she could contribute to the temple fund, she would donate as much as she was spending on her cigarettes.

The bishop commended her for her generosity but asked her to promise to quit smoking and to give the money she would have spent on cigarettes to the temple fund. In that setting she found the courage to promise to quit. With great enthusiasm, the woman, her daughter, and her bishop knelt in prayer to thank the Lord for his inspiration and to ask for his help.[12]

7. Repent

The youth of four New Mexico stakes helped prepare the Albuquerque temple site for groundbreaking. The teens brought shovels, rakes, and gloves to rid the site of cactus, sagebrush, weeds, and garbage. One young volunteer saw deep meaning in the efforts to prepare the temple site. "It's very symbolic," she said. "You have to be clean yourself to go to the temple." A young man who was awaiting his mission call, added, "We need to clean all the cactuses out of our lives before we can go to the temple."[13]

No one is immune to sin. At times each of us has "to clean all the cactuses out of our lives" through repentance.

A highlight of my life was attending the Kona Hawaii Temple dedication. I arrived at the temple two days before the dedication to research the temple's history and to take reference photographs for my artwork. Since President Hinckley wasn't scheduled to arrive for two more days, I fully expected to find few people on the temple grounds. I was surprised to see hundreds of people still working on the temple, preparing for its dedication ceremonies.

While visiting with the temple architect, I asked him what work remained. He told me workers still needed to polish the marble. He explained that they wanted to make it sparkle for the dedication. I sometimes think about this experience and how it relates to each of us, whether we are attending the temple for the first time or have previously been endowed. Just as workers undertook a great effort to make the Kona Temple sparkle, we should make a great effort to make our spirits and bodies perfectly clean.

Since no unclean thing can enter into the kingdom of God (1 Nephi 15:34), we should prepare to enter the temple

Kona

by taking a personal inventory of our lives and worthiness. It is by repenting that we polish the dirt of sin off our bodily temples and become worthy to enter the Lord's house.

You may be tempted to think that you have gone too far to repent. But President Hinckley, referring to the Savior's atonement, has given this encouraging counsel: "Now, if there be any who have stepped over the line, who may already have transgressed, is there any hope for you? Of course there is. Where there is true repentance, there will be forgiveness. That process begins with prayer. The Lord has said, 'He who has repented of his sins, the same is forgiven, and I, the Lord, remember them no more' (D&C 58:42). Share your burden with your parents if you can. And by all means, confess to your bishop, who stands ready to help you."[14]

While serving as the Salt Lake Temple president, Carlos E. Asay gave the following wise counsel on what it means to be

46

temple worthy. "Some might judge themselves too harshly; others might be too lenient. That is where the bishop and the temple recommend interview enter the picture. They help you measure yourself against the basic standards that have been set. You do not have to be perfect to enter the temple—the temple is there to help us become perfect. The Church member who is living the basic laws such as chastity, tithing, and the Word of Wisdom, and who answers the interview questions honestly, should feel worthy to enter the house of the Lord.

"You must be consistent in your righteousness and strive to attain a state of goodness whereby you will feel comfortable in God's holy house. Bear in mind that all of us will stand before the Lord one day—ready or not—to be judged (see Alma 42:1–31). The temple becomes a place where we prepare to meet the one who gave us life."[15]

It may be some years before you are old enough to receive temple ordinances, but preparing to go to the temple can still be a part of your everyday life. If you become discouraged, if temptations seem too strong, if living all of the gospel principles seems impossible, remember the powerful words of Nephi: "I will go and do the things which the Lord hath commanded, for I know that the Lord giveth no commandments unto the children of men, save he shall prepare a way for them that they may accomplish the thing which he commandeth them" (1 Nephi 3:7). When you face opposition, look for the way that the Lord has prepared for you to overcome the trial. Start living worthily for your temple blessings today. You can do it!

Young Latter-day Saints in Brazil provide a good example of how we can keep our temples pure even while living in a society that glorifies sin. An article published in the *Liahona*, the Church's international magazine, described the trials Brazilian youth frequently face: "They are teased by their peers if they don't use drugs, alcohol, and tobacco. Extreme immodesty is common on billboards and prime-time television. Many students carry pornographic magazines to school. During *carnival*, a famous weeklong festival in Brazil, immodesty and immorality parade in the streets.

"But Latter-day Saint youth say that looking to the temple helps them keep the commandments despite the many temptations and trials they face. 'At school, when you won't look at the [pornographic] magazines, people make fun of you. But I have a goal to serve a mission and marry in the temple, so I already know that if they push this stuff at me, I won't do it,' says Fabio Marques, age 16, of the Campinas Fourth Ward, Campinas Brazil Stake. 'I've already made my decision.'

"Fabio says having a temple so close to his home in Campinas will strengthen him and his Latter-day Saint friends. 'It's hard to get to the temple in São Paulo, but soon we'll be able to do baptisms for the dead more easily and frequently at the Campinas temple. And each time you do that, you make a stronger goal to return to the temple and to be worthy to marry in the temple.' "[16]

Regardless of what those in the world may do around you, you can make the decision to remain faithful to the commandments. Wherever you may live, the Lord will provide a way for you to overcome trials. Remember, your body is a temple. Commit now to a lifestyle that will keep your temple clean and pure. When necessary, follow the steps of repentance to polish the dirt of sin from your bodily temple. Be grateful for the commandments and for the gospel. They are the road map that will lead us to joy, to the temple, and back into the presence of our loving Heavenly Father.

NOTES

1. Olsen, *The Logan Temple*, 152–53.
2. Gordon B. Hinckley, "A Prophet's Counsel and Prayer for Youth," *New Era*, January 2001, 11.
3. Benson, *The Teachings of Ezra Taft Benson*, 284.
4. Robert K. Dellenbach, "Profanity," *New Era*, May 1992, 46.
5. Dellenbach, 49.
6. *For the Strength of Youth*, 17.
7. Hinckley, 11.
8. "Q&A: Questions and Answers," *New Era*, February 2000, 16, 18.
9. Ezra Taft Benson, "To the Youth of the Noble Birthright," *Ensign*, May 1986, 45.
10. George Tate, interview by author, tape recording, 5 September 2000, Las Vegas, Nevada.
11. Benson, *So Shall Ye Reap*, 172.
12. McKay, *For His House*, 13.
13. Shanna Ghaznavi, "A Site to Behold," *New Era*, November 1998, 14.
14. Hinckley, 13.
15. Carlos E. Asay, "The Temple: The Place for You," *New Era*, March 1997, 7–8.
16. Barbara Jean Jones, "Lives under Construction," *Liahona*, November, 2000, 11–12.

4

REDEEMING THE DEAD

Redeeming the dead is part of the great labor of love performed in the temple by the living in behalf of the dead. Eight young pioneer women demonstrated this love through strong faith and resolve to perform baptisms for the dead in the Logan Utah Temple. They started their trek to the temple at 4 A.M. During their journey, they had problems with all four wheels of their buggy. One came off entirely. Nevertheless, they repaired the wheels and continued on their journey. Other problems arose that also delayed them. Before they reached Logan, nearly every important part of their buggy had broken down. Despite their early start, they didn't reach the

temple that day until 5 P.M., after the font had been emptied. Temple workers who were still there, however, agreed to refill the font so that these faithful young women could be baptized for the dead.[1]

The history of vicarious work in this dispensation began with the building of the Kirtland Temple. The temple had no baptismal font because the revelation on baptism for the dead had not yet been given to the Prophet Joseph Smith. It wasn't until April 3, 1836, that Elijah appeared in the recently completed Kirtland Temple to commit "the keys of this dispensation" to Joseph Smith and Oliver Cowdery. Elijah is the Old

Testament prophet who, as prophesied in the scriptures, would return to earth to begin a mighty work.

Elijah's mission was so important that the prophecy concerning his appearance is repeated, with only slight variations, in each of the books of scripture the Lord has given to us: "Behold, I will send you Elijah the prophet before the coming of the great and dreadful day of the Lord: And he shall turn the heart of the fathers to the children, and the heart of the children to their fathers, lest I come and smite the earth with a curse" (Malachi 4:5–6; 3 Nephi 25:5–6; D&C 2; JS–H 1:38–39).

During the early days of the Restoration, the Lord said, "Remember the worth of souls is great in the sight of God" (D&C 18:10). Nothing testifies more strongly to this truth than the work that goes on in the temples for both the living and the dead.

The ordinance of vicarious baptism for the dead was first taught in this dispensation after the Saints settled in Nauvoo. The Prophet Joseph Smith indicated that the Saints could "now act for their friends who had departed this life, and that the plan of salvation was calculated to save all who were willing to obey the requirements of the law of God."[2] Members of the Church demonstrated their enthusiasm and faith almost immediately by performing vicarious baptisms in the Mississippi River.

After a time, the Lord declared that the ordinance of baptism for the dead "belongeth to my house," and that he had temporarily allowed the Saints to perform this ordinance outside the temple "only in the days of [their] poverty" (D&C 124:30). Baptisms for the dead continued in the Mississippi River until the Nauvoo Temple was sufficiently completed to

allow for the performing of this ordinance. While the temple was still being constructed, the baptistry was covered by a temporary roof and dedicated by Joseph Smith on November 8, 1841. By the summer of 1844, when the Prophet was martyred, the Saints had performed 15,722 vicarious baptisms.[3]

"The greatest responsibility in this world that God has laid upon us is to seek after our dead," the Prophet Joseph Smith said. He later taught, "It is not only necessary that you should be baptized for your dead, but you will have to go through all the ordinances for them, the same as you have gone through to save yourselves."[4] Since that time, latter-day prophets have repeatedly reminded us of our obligations to serve in the temple in behalf of our ancestors.

The belief that the living may officiate in saving ordinances for the dead sets The Church of Jesus Christ of Latter-day Saints apart from all other religions. When you go to the temple, you go as a servant of the Lord to do work that is vital for the salvation of those who have passed on without receiving saving ordinances. The deceased in the spirit world may then choose to accept or reject the ordinance.

Many beyond the veil eagerly await the completion of their temple work, as revealed to President Wilford Woodruff in the St. George Utah Temple. He was in the temple late one evening when the spirits of many of America's founding fathers gathered around him.

"Every one of those men that signed the Declaration of Independence, with General Washington, called upon me . . .

two consecutive nights, and demanded at my hands that I should go forth and attend to the ordinances of the House of God for them,"⁵ said President Woodruff. As a result, temple work was completed for the founders, as well as for other prominent historical figures.

RESEARCHING YOUR FAMILY HISTORY

To do temple work in behalf of our ancestors, we must first identify them. We do this through family history research. Once you have gathered the names of your ancestors, you can send or take those names to the temple for vicarious work. Many young people ignore this responsibility and blessing, leaving it to their parents or other relatives to do the research. But those who have learned to do this research are excited to be involved.

It is one thing to serve vicariously in behalf of a stranger but quite another to participate in behalf of an ancestor you have come to know through your research. Imagine the joy involved in helping deceased relatives receive saving ordinances and be sealed together in family units!

For some, mention of family history or the word *genealogy* conjures up images of sitting in a dingy library, endlessly looking through volumes of old, dusty manuscripts in a search that leads nowhere. But family history research involves much more than merely writing down names, dates, places, and statistics. Family history research involves learning about real people and their trials and triumphs, and it is another way you can make the temple a part of your daily life.

Many of your forebears lived a harder life than you can even imagine. As you discover the sacrifices they made and the hardships they endured, chances are you'll discover inspiring examples of courage and faithful endurance. Your ancestors can be great role models for you.

Researching your family history, therefore, can be fun and meaningful, and you needn't be an expert to make contributions. Once you learn basic research skills, your efforts will become an adventure as you hunt for names, dates, and details. While doing your detective work, you will begin to feel a connection with your relatives as you find similarities between your life and theirs. As you serve your ancestors, you'll learn that you're doing more than just research—you're helping loved ones progress toward eternal salvation.

Latter-day Saint youth around the world are reaping blessings as they actively participate in researching their family history. In Brazil, for example, the São Paulo Brazil Temple accommodates busload after busload of adults and youth by remaining open all night on Friday and late on Saturday.

In an article in the *Liahona*, former São Paulo temple president Aledir Barbour cited "a group of youth and their leaders who traveled by bus from Belo Horizonte, a large city about 200 kilometers northeast of São Paulo. Youth from this stake brought with them the names of 10,000 ancestors, all of whom the teens had identified through their own research. The group stayed from Tuesday to Friday, but it wasn't nearly enough time to perform the baptisms for all their ancestors."[6]

The most important step in doing family history research is the first one—getting started. Today you have the advantages of being able to research using a personal computer, working in a family history library, and using the Internet. You can even go to the Church's website, www.familysearch.com, and find a tutorial called Research Guidance that will lead you through the research process. Also, your stake likely has a family history consultant who can help you.

One of the sweet rewards of gathering information about our ancestors is performing vicarious baptisms for those whose names we find. In Nicaragua, a group of young women researched and prepared records on their respective family histories and then financially sacrificed to serve their ancestors in the temple. This "group of 49 young women and their leaders took 2,000 names to the Guatemala City Temple. It took each girl a year to save enough money to go. These faithful young women rode a bus almost two days' journey through

three country borders and spent two or three days at the temple before returning home."[7] They learned of the beautiful feeling that comes in knowing that we are helping further Heavenly Father's work.

In Salt Lake City, one young woman described her experience with family history by saying, "After doing the research, the reward is being baptized and knowing you're helping that person. It is extra special when you can be baptized for someone you've found."[8] These blessings are available to almost anyone who takes family history seriously. Participating in this marvelous work will strengthen your testimony and help you prepare for further blessings awaiting you in the temple.

KEEPING A JOURNAL

As temples are built, a temple historian is given the responsibility to record all events pertaining to the temple's history. When the temple is dedicated, a copy of this precious history is included in the items permanently placed within the temple's cornerstone. In like manner, you have the opportunity to record your own precious history by keeping a journal.

I began to understand the importance of keeping a journal while serving as a missionary. At the beginning of my mission I promised myself that I would keep a record of those important two years of my life by writing in my journal every day. I achieved that goal, though on some days I wrote only one sentence. As details from my mission fade from my memory, I can rekindle them by reading my mission journal. I made one of my most special journal entries on June 12, 1992. I had been a missionary for only a short time and was in the meetinghouse in Kaiserslautern, Germany, memorizing the first discussion in German. I recorded the following:

"Tonight my companion and I met an investigator at the meetinghouse for a baptismal interview. We entered and were the only ones in the entire building. As my companion and the investigator met in a private room, I sat out in the hallway and began to memorize Joseph Smith's First Vision. I started by saying a prayer. As I recited the Prophet's vision account in German, I really had a special experience. Without expecting it, the Spirit came over me and I felt a warmth throughout my body. I did not want to be distracted, so I closed my eyes and savored this confirmation that Joseph Smith is a true prophet. I then sang to myself the hymn, 'Joseph Smith's First Prayer,' and my testimony grew. The gospel is true and I am so grateful to be a missionary!" This personal witness blessed me throughout my mission, and because I recorded it in my journal, it continues to be a strength to me today.

The most valuable records ever kept—the scriptures—were written by individuals about their lives and are much like journals. Your journal may be read by only a few people, but the words you record will become a precious treasure to you and your family. Writing in your journal can also be fun. When trying to decide what to write, simply ask yourself what you wish you knew about a favorite ancestor. Then record those types of things from your own life. They might include your thoughts on world events, your priesthood blessings, and your testimony.

Though you shouldn't dwell on failures and disappointments, you might want to keep a record of them and of what you learned from them. After all, we all have them, and your grandchildren will probably be able to relate to you better if they don't think you lived a perfect life.

Writing in your journal is an important way to prepare yourself for the temple. It is a way of strengthening family ties for past and future generations, and it turns "the heart of the fathers to the children, and the heart of the children to their fathers" (Malachi 4:6). President Spencer W. Kimball explained one of the greatest benefits of keeping a journal when he said, "Those who keep a personal journal are more likely to keep the Lord in remembrance in their daily lives."[9]

PERFORMING BAPTISMS FOR THE DEAD

If you are a Latter-day Saint over the age of twelve, you may obtain your own temple recommend. (Children under twelve may enter the temple only to be sealed to their parents.) A temple recommend, good for a year, entitles you to enter the temple and perform baptisms for the dead. Wouldn't it be a wonderful goal for you to always be worthy to hold a temple recommend, starting at the age of twelve?

When performing baptisms for the dead, you will feel the joy that comes from opening the door for someone to accept the gospel. You may perform baptisms for the dead individually or in groups arranged by the bishop or branch president. If you haven't had the opportunity to perform this ordinance, talk to your bishop, who will then assist you in visiting the temple.

During my mission to Frankfurt, Germany, I had the privilege of serving with Elder Andreas Kleinert. Elder Kleinert was raised in the communistic environment of the former East Germany. He showed his testimony of temple service a few

months after the Freiberg Germany Temple was dedicated in July 1985. Temple president Henry Burkhardt discovered early one morning that baptisms had not been performed for 108 males scheduled for ordinance work that day. He felt that the ordinance work should not be interrupted even though the heating system was off and the water in the baptismal font was icy cold. He called Andreas Kleinert, then a fourteen-year-old Aaronic Priesthood holder who lived nearby. Thirty minutes later, Andreas and President Burkhardt entered the freezing water.

"When I was immersed for the first time, it felt like I was rolling in snow," said Andreas. "I just could not get used to the cold water." He and President Burkhardt were determined to

continue, however, and worked until all 108 baptisms had been performed. "Never had I shivered like this before," Andreas said. "But . . . neither President Burkhardt nor I even caught a cold. I was happy that I was once again able to do work in the temple for the dead."[10]

President Howard W. Hunter counseled members of the Church to attend the temple often. "We should hasten to the temple as frequently, yet prudently, as our personal circumstances allow," he said.[11] This counsel applies to both young and old in the Church. The responsibility, however, is left to each of us to decide how frequently we visit the Lord's house. Although some Latter-day Saints may be too young to visit a temple on their own or may live a great distance from the nearest temple, the important thing is to follow the prophet's counsel by going as often as possible.

Although they were hundreds of miles from the nearest temple, a group of young men living outside Montreal, Canada, undertook a "sweet" project to finance a trip to the Washington D.C. Temple. They cared for eighty-three bee-hives and assisted in processing honey, for which they received a daily salary of a bucket of honey. Other young people in the local ward then did their part by packaging and selling the honey to earn money for the temple trip. The young men and young women showed by their hard work their enthusiasm to attend the temple.

Washington D.C.

Seventeen–year-old Frankie Belot said, "We tell the people who walk by our stand that we're raising money for a trip to our temple. We show them a picture of the temple and tell them what it means to us." Regarding her desires to attend the temple, fifteen-year-old Sonya Roy said, "We want to be baptized for those people who've died without being introduced to the Church."[12]

When she was nineteen, my wife's sister, Suzanne Cederlof, made a commitment to regularly perform baptisms for the dead. "Two years ago I made the goal to attend the temple once a week to perform baptisms for the dead," she said. "That decision greatly changed my life. I feel closer to my Father in Heaven than ever before and feel increased peace and happiness. I love being baptized for women who have gone before me. On some occasions, I have felt a tangible closeness to them. It's almost as though I can feel their excitement at becoming newly baptized members of the Church. When I enter the temple, it's as if I'm walking through the doors of heaven, and suddenly my worldly concerns seem to melt away. It is nearly impossible to describe the joy I feel and the way my testimony has grown."

Tremendous blessings await us if we unselfishly serve in the temple. We will experience the joy that comes from serving others while serving our God (Mosiah 2:17). As we faithfully serve the Lord, he will strengthen us to put off the natural man.

You have the glorious opportunity of performing ordinances for your ancestors that they cannot do for themselves. You can identify these individuals from your research and then submit their names to the temple. When obstacles and distractions arise to prevent you from participating in family history work or performing temple service, do not give up! Reach your goal by repairing the wagon wheel and continuing on your journey. As you do your part, the Lord will bless and assist you.

NOTES

1. Olsen, *Logan Temple*, 166.
2. Cowan, *Temples to Dot the Earth*, 45.
3. Cowan, 46.
4. Smith, *History of the Church*, 6:313, 365.
5. Conference Report, April 1898, 89–90.
6. Barbara Jean Jones, "Lives under Construction," *Liahona*, November 2000, 8.
7. Carol B. Thomas, "Preparing Our Families for the Temple," *Ensign*, May 1999, 12.
8. Lori Stephenson Dawson, "Even in an Ordinary Ward," *New Era*, November 1987, 11.
9. Spencer W. Kimball, "President Kimball Speaks Out on Personal Journals," *New Era*, December 1980, 26–27.
10. "Hero in the Font," *Church News*, 14 February 1987, 16.
11. Howard W. Hunter, "A Temple-Motivated People," *Ensign*, February 1995, 2.
12. Kathleen Lubeck, "Sweet Is the Work," *New Era*, February 1989, 28–31.

PART TWO

PREPARING FOR THE TEMPLE

___

TEMPLE MARRIAGE

___

TEMPLE QUESTIONS AND ANSWERS

___

5

PREPARING FOR THE TEMPLE

As the youngest of four children, I was not old enough to attend any of my siblings' temple marriages. I remember feeling sad because I couldn't be more involved in those special events, but I am grateful for the wonderful example my brothers and sister set for me. While my sister was being married in the Idaho Falls Idaho Temple, I sat outside on the temple steps, thinking that temples were for adults only and no place for a young boy like me. I have since learned that I was wrong.

Though children can't participate in all the ordinances of the temple, the temple remains a special place for every one of Heavenly Father's worthy children—the young, middle-aged, and elderly. A person is never too young or too old to become acquainted with the Lord. Samuel of the Old Testament was only a boy when he was called into the service of the Lord, and Joseph Smith was just fourteen when he experienced the First Vision. Jesus revealed his special love for children when he said, "Suffer the little children to come unto me, and forbid them not: for of such is the kingdom of God" (Mark 10:14).

Although your first trip to the temple may seem far off, you should begin preparing now. Curiosity or deep interest alone does not constitute preparation. In a *New Era* article, Kathleen Lubeck described temple preparation as "a process, not a one-time event," and she quoted some sound advice from several former temple presidents. "There's no such thing as a crash course for going to the temple," said one. "A person needs to have a testimony. If he has a testimony of God's eternal plan he won't be satisfied with anything but having the temple be a part of his life."[1]

Another former temple president suggested that young people "take advantage of Church programs and the opportunity to respond to leadership callings." And a third said it's important that they attend the temple for the right reasons. "If young people come to the temple for the wrong reasons, like family or peer pressure, they usually don't have a desire to come back. If they go with the right spirit, they'll be hungering and thirsting and wanting to find out all they can about what's taught in the temple."[2]

It's appropriate that you discuss your approaching temple

experience with your parents or bishop. Though much of what we do in the temple is not to be discussed outside the temple, you should know certain things as you prepare to go for the first time. Some of your questions can be answered in greater detail during special "temple recommend" interviews with your bishop and stake president. The first requirement for holding a temple recommend is worthiness. That is something you should be working on right now by striving to be honest and morally clean, live the Word of Wisdom, avoid bad language, attend your meetings, and support Church leaders. If you have any doubt about these standards, review them by reading the *For the Strength of Youth* booklet.

THE ENDOWMENT

A temple recommend entitles you to enter the temple to perform baptisms for the dead after you turn twelve. When you're old enough to serve a mission or be married, the next ordinance you prepare for is your endowment. In a worldly sense, an endowment is a gift. You might read in the newspaper or hear on TV that a wealthy person has "endowed" a university or a museum or a symphony orchestra. That simply means the person has given that institution something of value, quite often money or property.

When you go to the temple to receive your endowment, the Lord will "endow" you with a precious gift—knowledge you need to work out your salvation and progress toward eternal life. Because that knowledge is sacred, we are instructed to keep it confidential—safe in our hearts and minds. Most young people receive their endowment after they've received a mission call, before reporting to the Missionary Training

Center, or before being married, or sealed, in the temple. Couples who have been married in a civil ceremony but who later wish to be sealed often receive their endowment just before their temple sealing.

What you gain from the temple will largely depend on how well you prepare beforehand. The covenants or promises you will make there are sacred. As you contemplate going to the temple, you should prepare yourself by making certain that you are worthy in every way. Those who rush their preparation or misrepresent their worthiness are less likely to understand the temple ceremony and to keep their sacred covenants. Because making covenants with the Lord is such a solemn and sacred thing, only those who are spiritually prepared should take part in temple ordinances.

UNDERSTANDING TEMPLE CEREMONIES

If you have read the Book of Mormon more than once, you know that your understanding of it increases with every reading. Even familiar scriptures can take on deeper meaning depending on your spiritual condition or life circumstances. Nephi counseled us to "feast upon the words of Christ; for behold, the words of Christ will tell you all things what ye should do" (2 Nephi 32:3). To feast is not to partake casually, lightly, or quickly. Feasting implies partaking deeply and extensively over a longer period of time.

Compare eating at a fast-food restaurant, where the goal is to quickly satisfy your appetite, to sitting down to a Thanksgiving dinner, where we eat more slowly, taking time to savor various dishes and flavors. To feast on the scriptures requires effort and humility as we read, ponder, and pray for

understanding and enlightenment. Something similar hap-
pens when we make repeated trips to the temple.

After we receive our endowment, we can return to the
temple to do endowment work for the dead. The endowment
ceremony is the same each time, but as we repeat it, we come
to a deeper understanding of what the Lord is trying to teach
us. That increased understanding can come to each of us if we
are prayerful and attentive and allow the Holy Ghost to tutor
us. To ensure that we are worthy of that kind of inspiration is
one reason we must renew our temple recommends annually.
Once a year we certify to our bishop and stake president that
we remain committed to keeping our covenants.

Following their first visit to the temple, most people admit
that they didn't understand everything they experienced.
That is because the ceremony is filled with symbols, which
have several different meanings. During his earthly ministry,
Jesus used this same technique to teach his gospel. He called

himself a good shepherd, compared his followers to sheep, and likened the gospel to a "pearl of great price" (Matthew 13:46). In a similar way, the endowment is filled with symbolism.

Temple workers know that those who are new to the temple do not understand everything that takes place, and they patiently guide and direct them through the experience. You don't need to fear being embarrassed or getting confused. The Lord teaches us by giving us as much information as we can absorb—"line upon line, precept upon precept" (D&C 98:12) until we gain a fullness of light and knowledge. Only

by returning to the temple again and again will you be blessed to understand its mysteries.³

Those who go to the temple regularly enjoy the feeling that the work they are doing is vitally important to those for whom they labor. They also enjoy expanding their understanding of the gospel and renewing their commitment to the Savior and his Church. It's exciting to know that as we return to the temple to feast upon the words of Christ, our testimonies and gospel understanding grow and our lives are blessed.

OVERCOMING OPPOSITION AS YOU PREPARE FOR THE TEMPLE

While serving a full-time mission, I learned that Satan uses all of his tricks to hinder the work of the Lord. As investigators made progress toward baptism, they would often begin experiencing trials that tested their faith and growing testimonies. We quickly learned to expect such opposition.

In a similar way, the adversary and his followers focus their efforts on righteous individuals who are trying to achieve their temple goals. A president of the Logan Utah Temple once warned that Satan and his followers will "whisper in the ears of the people, persuading them not to go to the Temple."⁴

Elder Boyd K. Packer has called temples "the very center of the spiritual strength of the Church. We should expect that the adversary will try to interfere with us as a Church and with us individually as we seek to participate in this sacred and inspired work. The interference can vary from the terrible persecutions of the earlier days to apathy toward the work. The latter is perhaps the most dangerous and debilitating form of resistance to temple work."⁵

It isn't uncommon for obstacles to arise that hinder temple attendance. I know of people who have had difficulty getting to the temple because of problems getting away from work, accidents at home, trouble finding baby-sitters, and car trouble.

Elder Glenn L. Pace was a witness to the troubles that hindered efforts to build a temple in West Africa. He said the adversary was behind the opposition and that Lucifer was "aware of the large number of Africans who have accepted the gospel on the other side of the veil and are anxiously awaiting their proxy baptism and temple endowment as well as being sealed to their families. When a temple is dedicated, the dam in the spirit world will break and there will be a flood of humanity who have lived on the African continent flow into the temple of the Lord as their descendants do their work for them. We should not be surprised that Lucifer is using every means at his disposal to keep a temple from these people."[6]

Since the early days of the Restoration, faithful Saints have faced and overcome opposition in order to receive blessings found only within the temple. While they built the Nauvoo Temple, many Saints suffered from poverty and sickness. Healthy Church members who could get work often worked for food alone. Nonetheless, the Church asked men to spend one day in ten working on the temple as "tithing in time." Brigham Young later noted that some of the workers on the temple had no shoes or shirts.[7]

Many skilled craftsmen worked full time on the temple without guarantee of compensation. One notable example was Charles Lambert, who had recently joined the Church and emigrated from England. Although he had the responsibility of providing for his wife and her orphaned sister and two

76

brothers, he pledged that he would continue to work until the temple was finished, regardless of whether he was paid for his services. One morning while Charles was walking along the street, a stranger stopped him and asked if his name was Charles Lambert. Charles replied that it was, and the stranger responded that his name was Higgins.

"I have heard of your skill as a workman, and want you to go to Missouri and work for me," the stranger said. "You are not appreciated or properly paid here. If you will quit the Temple and go and work for me, you can name your own price and you will be sure of your pay."

Charles thanked the man for the offer but declined. He then bade the stranger farewell, wondering how the man had known his name and heard of his skill. Charles turned to look again at the stranger but could see him nowhere. He had disappeared. Brother Lambert pledged to continue serving the Lord by working on the temple regardless of payment. This commitment gave him the strength to remain faithful when the adversary later tempted him.[8]

The scriptures teach "that there is an opposition in all

things" (2 Nephi 2:11). As you do your best to prepare for the temple, expect temptations and trials. Your trials will be different from Brother Lambert's, but you can demonstrate your faithfulness on a daily basis at school and work, and with family and friends. Pledge to yourself now that you will be faithful to the Lord's commandments. You will then be like Brother Lambert, having strength to overcome challenges that could prevent you from obtaining temple blessings.

UNDERSTANDING THE LANGUAGE OF THE TEMPLE

When I was a twenty-year-old missionary, a sixty-five-year-old man asked me why he should call me *Elder*. At the time, the elderly man and I did not share the same definition of the word. Examples of the distinct nature of our gospel language abound. For example, only a member of the Church would understand why a three-year-old child would be called a *Sunbeam*, that we occasionally attend *firesides* inside a chapel, and that we sometimes attend church at a *stake center*.

Do you remember being confused when you tried to read the Bible or the Book of Mormon for the first time? Your confusion probably resulted from reading many unfamiliar scriptural words and phrases. But as you became more familiar with the language of the scriptures, you comprehended more. In a similar way, the temple has its own unique language. For example, if you didn't understand work in behalf of the dead, you could become confused like the young boy who overheard his parents say they were going to the temple to do sealings. "Are you going to do the walls too?" he asked.

The following word definitions will help you understand

more fully what you need to know as you prepare for the temple.

Covenants. Members of The Church of Jesus Christ of Latter-day Saints are often described as "a covenant people." In the temple, Latter-day Saints enter into the most sacred covenants they make. "A covenant is a bond; a solemn agreement. It involves at least two individuals, and, of course, both parties must abide by the conditions of the covenant in order to make it effective and binding. The gospel in its fullness, as it has been restored, is the new and everlasting covenant of God."[9]

Elder Bruce R. McConkie taught that being baptized, partaking of the sacrament, paying tithing, keeping the Sabbath holy, and observing the Word of Wisdom are all examples of covenants. The Lord has promised us specific blessings in return for our observance of these laws. "The more faithful and devoted a person is, the more . . . covenants of the Lord he is enabled to receive," Elder McConkie added.[10] By keeping our covenants, we find joy in this life and eternal blessings in the life to come.

Degree of glory. Because we perform at different levels during our earthly probation, we receive customized heavenly rewards after we die. With reference to this, the apostle Paul wrote, "There are also celestial bodies, and bodies terrestrial: but the glory of the celestial is one, and the glory of the terrestrial is another. There is one glory of the sun, and another glory of the moon, and another glory of the stars: for one star differeth from another star in glory" (1 Corinthians 15:40–42). The exterior stonework of some of our temples features images of the sun, moon, and stars.

Endowment. In the temple, as discussed earlier, we receive an endowment, which is literally a gift from our Heavenly Father. President Brigham Young taught, "Your endowment is, to receive all those ordinances in the House of the Lord, which are necessary for you, after you have departed this life, to enable you to walk back to the presence of the Father, passing the angels who stand as sentinels, being enabled to . . . gain your eternal exaltation."[11]

Eternal life. "Eternal life is exaltation in the highest heaven—the kind of life that God lives."[12] Celestial marriage is the gate to exaltation and eternal life, which consists of eternal increase and the continuation of the family unit.[13]

Initiatory ordinances. You receive the initiatory ordinances of washing and anointing before you receive your endowment. "In connection with these ordinances, in the temple you will be officially clothed in the garment and promised marvelous

blessings in connection with it. It is important that you listen carefully as these ordinances are administered and that you try to remember the blessings promised and the conditions upon which they will be realized."[14]

Keys. Elder Boyd K. Packer said, "We use the word *keys* in a symbolic way. Here the keys of priesthood authority represent the limits of the power extended from beyond the veil to mortal man to act in the name of God upon the earth. The words *seal* and *keys* and *priesthood* are closely linked together."[15]

Referring to the keys of the priesthood, President Joseph F. Smith said, "The priesthood in general is the authority given to man to act for God. Every man ordained to any degree of the priesthood has this authority delegated to him. But it is necessary that every act performed under this authority shall be done at the proper time and place, in the proper way, and after the proper order. The power of directing these labors constitutes the keys of the priesthood. In their fullness, the keys are held by only one person at a time, the prophet and President of the Church. He may delegate any portion of this power to another, in which case that person holds the keys of that particular labor."[16]

Ordinances. The work we perform in the temple centers on several ordinances. These sacred rites, for us and for our departed ancestors, bind us in a special way to each other and to our Heavenly Father. They are essential to our salvation. Without them, President Gordon B. Hinckley has taught, the gospel is incomplete.[17]

"Ordinances and covenants become our credentials for admission into [God's] presence," said Elder Boyd K. Packer.

"To worthily receive them is the quest of a lifetime; to keep them thereafter is the challenge of mortality."[18]

Patron. A temple patron is any member of the Church who attends the temple to perform ordinances.

Prayer roll. Each temple maintains a list called a prayer roll. Names may be placed on these rolls by temple patrons or by Church members via telephone. Those whose names are included typically face such burdens as sickness, affliction, or difficult decisions or challenges. Special prayers are offered in the temple in behalf of these people.

Proxy. A proxy is someone who acts or serves as a substitute or surrogate for another. In the temple, patrons serve as proxies for those who have died without an opportunity in this life to receive saving ordinances. Because temple ordinances are always presented in the same way, patrons review covenants and teachings as they officiate for someone who is deceased.

Sealing power. On April 3, 1836, the prophet Elijah appeared in the Kirtland Temple and conferred upon Joseph Smith the power to perform sealing ordinances that will be recognized in heaven (D&C 110:13–16). President Gordon B. Hinckley described this sealing power as "unique and wonderful. It is the authority exercised in the temples of God. It concerns both the living and the dead. It is of the very essence of eternity. It is divine power bestowed by the Almighty as a part of His great plan for the immortality and eternal life of man."[19]

Sealings. Elder McConkie described sealings as "those ordinances performed in the temples whereby husbands and wives are sealed together in the marriage union for time and eternity, and whereby children are sealed eternally to parents."[20]

Symbols. The Lord frequently chooses to teach us through symbols. The temple itself is a symbol.

"Each temple is a house of learning. There we are taught in the Master's way. His way differs from modes of others. His way is ancient and rich with symbolism. We can learn much by pondering the reality for which each symbol stands. Teachings of the temple are beautifully simple and simply beautiful. They are understood by the humble, yet they can excite the intellect of the brightest minds."[21]

President Howard W. Hunter encouraged us "look to the temple of the Lord as the great symbol of [our] membership."[22] The temple may be likened unto a shining beacon in a world of darkness. Following the light of this beacon will lead us to the safety found only in the gospel of Jesus Christ.

Temple garment. After Latter-day Saints receive their temple ordinances, they then wear the special temple garment or underclothing. The garment does not prevent you from wearing fashionable modest clothing. "As you receive your endowments in the temple, you receive the privilege of wearing the sacred temple clothing and the garments of the holy priesthood," said Elder J. Richard Clarke. "The garments are a tangible reminder of your covenants with God. It has been said that modesty is the hallmark of a true Latter-day Saint. The temple garment reminds us that virtue sets us apart from the world and, in a special way, makes us one with God."[23]

The First Presidency has stated, "Endowed members of the Church wear the garment as a reminder of the sacred covenants they have made with the Lord and also as a protection against temptation and evil. How it is worn is an outward expression of an inward commitment to follow the Savior."[24]

Vicarious service. Vicarious service is service rendered in behalf of someone else. Much of the work done in the temples is vicarious service, performed by the living in behalf of the dead. Such service enables departed souls to receive ordinances necessary for salvation and exaltation.

RECEIVING A TEMPLE RECOMMEND

To be admitted to the temple, you must have a current temple recommend. A temple recommend certifies that you have been interviewed by your bishop and a member of the stake presidency and affirms that you are worthy and are keeping the commandments. You don't need to fear these interviews. Your priesthood leaders will help you determine your worthiness and readiness, and they will answer any questions you may have. In this responsibility, they represent the Lord. You need to answer their questions honestly. Lying to your leaders in order to gain entrance to the temple is like lying to the Lord.

"To misrepresent our worthiness to our bishop and receive a recommend dishonestly denies us the blessings of the temple," said Elder Clarke. "We cannot fool the Lord, who will not honor false credentials."[25]

Holding a temple recommend is a priceless privilege and reminds us as we enter the temple that we do so as the Lord's guest. President Howard W. Hunter said that to qualify for a temple recommend we must

- "Believe in God the Eternal Father, in his Son Jesus Christ, and in the Holy Ghost."
- "Sustain the General Authorities and local authorities of the Church."

84

- "Be morally clean."
- "Ensure that there is nothing in your relationship with family members that is out of harmony with the teachings of the Church."
- "Be honest in all of your dealings with others."
- "Strive to do your duty in the Church, attending your sacrament, priesthood, and other meetings."
- "Be a full-tithe payer and live the Word of Wisdom."[26]

A temple recommend is valid for a year and must be renewed annually. Renewing your recommend gives you the opportunity to sit down every year with your bishop and stake president and reevaluate your worthiness. Your goal should be worthiness to always hold a temple recommend.

"I have here my temple recommend," President Hinckley told Church members in Guadalajara, Mexico. "To me, it is a very precious and wonderful thing. I urge each one of you who is an adult in this Church to go to your bishop and get a temple recommend, and carry it in your pocket once again, and look upon it, and think what it means. It says, 'I have been to my bishop. I have been to my stake president. They have interviewed me and they have found me worthy as a member of this Church. I have a testimony of its truths. I sustain its officers. I am kind and dear to my family. I live the Word of Wisdom. I pay my tithing, and I am proud to be a faithful member of the Church.' Brethren and sisters, get a temple recommend and let it influence your behavior as a member of this Church."[27]

To make a temple recommend valid, you must sign it. By so doing so, you certify to the Lord that you are worthy of the privilege and blessings granted to those holding a temple recommend.

WHAT YOU CAN DO TODAY TO PREPARE FOR THE TEMPLE

Here are some things you can do to begin preparing for the temple:

- Read the books of Moses and Abraham in the Pearl of Great Price.
- Invite your bishop to explain to your ward's young men and young women what it means to be temple worthy. Ask him to review the temple recommend questions with you.
- Hang a picture of a temple in your bedroom, on your bathroom mirror, or in your school locker. This picture will serve as a daily reminder of your commitment to prepare for the temple and keep your baptismal covenants. It will remind you that by making the right choices, you'll be worthy to live forever with your Heavenly Father, your Savior, and your family.
- Make personal prayer and scripture study a daily practice.
- Wear modest clothing so that you don't have to make any drastic wardrobe changes after going to the temple. Dressing modestly also shows that you respect the sacredness of your body.
- Complete your family history group sheet, and find and submit names of ancestors for ordinance work. Doing temple work for your ancestors will make your temple experience even more meaningful and exciting.
- If your parents have been to the temple, ask them to explain what the temple means to them. Ask them what they remember most about the day they were sealed.

- Begin a journal. List the reasons you want to experience temple blessings, and record spiritual experiences.
- Be ready to enter the temple at all times. If there is anything in your life that makes you unworthy of the temple, do "not procrastinate the day of your repentance" (Alma 13:27). Talk with your bishop and let him help you repent.
- If you are twelve or older, meet with your bishop or branch president to obtain a youth temple recommend. Plan on being worthy to hold a temple recommend for the rest of your life.
- Review your baptismal covenants and honor them. Being true to your commitment to the Lord will prepare you for the additional covenants you will make in the temple.
- Choose friends who share your enthusiasm for the gospel and who desire to remain clean and virtuous. Date only those who have spiritual goals similar to yours.
- Decide now to be married in the temple. As you face trials or temptations, think about what you'll be giving up if you fail to keep yourself worthy.

WHAT TO EXPECT DURING YOUR FIRST TEMPLE VISIT

Arrive early. Arriving ahead of time, especially on your first visit, allows you to enter the Lord's house with an unhurried feeling. When I am asked to speak at a stake fireside or institute devotional, I like to be the first one there. This allows me time to cast aside my cares and reflect on how I might personalize my message for my audience. Without fail, these extra moments help me deliver a more meaningful presentation.

Likewise, you should do your best to allow ample time for your visits to the temple. By doing so, you prepare yourself to be taught by the Spirit in the house of the Lord.

As you attend the temple for the first time, you will probably be a little nervous. This is normal. After all, you are going to experience something you have anticipated for a long time. I remember that my friends and I, while preparing for our missions, were a little nervous about going to the temple for the first time. But my nervousness disappeared as soon as I walked through the temple doors and was greeted by smiling temple workers. They were kind and patient, and they assisted and guided me at every turn.

When visiting the Lord's house, wear clean, well-maintained clothing similar to what you might wear to sacrament meeting. Because you won't want to do anything to detract from the peace and beauty of the setting, avoid extreme fashions or hairstyles. While there, be reverent and attentive, and speak in soft tones.

Temple preparation requires effort and time. By honoring your baptismal covenants now, you are preparing to make temple covenants in the future. As you prepare for the temple, do so with peace and comfort in your heart. Everything in the temple is beautiful, uplifting, and sanctifying. You have nothing to fear.

Be worthy and go to the temple with maturity, dignity, and gratitude. Always remember that you are a guest and that it is a privilege to go to the house of the Lord.

NOTES

1. Kathleen Lubeck, "Preparing for the Temple Endowment," *New Era*, February 1987, 11.

2. Lubeck, 11.

3. Packer, *The Holy Temple*, 41–42.

4. "Genealogical Department," *Deseret News*, Church Department, 12 December 1936, 8.

5. Packer, 177.

6. Glenn L. Pace, "A Temple for West Africa," *Ensign*, May 2000, 26.

7. Cowan, *Temples to Dot the Earth*, 52.

8. Cannon, *Gems of Reminiscence*, 173–75.

9. ElRay L. Christiansen, Conference Report, April 1955, 28–29.

10. McConkie, *Mormon Doctrine*, 167.

11. Young, *Discourses of Brigham Young*, 416.

12. Russell M. Nelson, "Personal Preparation for Temple Blessings," *Ensign*, May 2001, 33.

13. McConkie, 257.

14. Packer, 155.

15. Packer, 82.

16. Smith, *Doctrines of Salvation*, 3:134.

17. "Messages from President Gordon B. Hinckley about Temple Work," *Deseret News 1999–2000 Church Almanac*, 479.

18. Packer, "Covenants," *Ensign*, May 1987, 24.

19. Hinckley, *Teachings of Gordon B. Hinckley*, 475.

20. McConkie, 684.

21. Nelson, 33.

22. Howard W. Hunter, "Exceeding Great and Precious Promises," *Ensign*, November 1994, 8.

23. J. Richard Clarke, "The Temple—What It Means to You," *New Era*, April 1993, 7.

24. Carlos E. Asay, "The Temple Garment: 'An Outward Expression of an Inward Commitment'" *Ensign*, August 1997, 22.

25. Clarke, 6.

26. Howard W. Hunter, "Your Temple Recommend," *New Era*, April 1995, 7, 8.

27. "Messages from President Gordon B. Hinckley about Temple Work," 479.

6

TEMPLE MARRIAGE

During my stay at the Missionary Training Center while preparing to serve a mission, we missionaries were allowed to attend the Provo Temple every preparation day. On one such occasion, I noticed a young couple that was about to enter the celestial room together for the first time. I was present, along with the couple's families and friends, when they entered the celestial room holding hands. They seemed to be unaware of anyone else in the room as they turned to each other and embraced. As I witnessed their joy, the Spirit touched my heart. I knew then that someday I wanted to be married in the temple and that I would accept no substitute for a temple marriage. I had always known it was the right thing to do, but I feel that the Lord allowed me that experience to strengthen my commitment and resolve.

Although people talk about loving someone enough to want to be with that person forever, love alone is not enough to make "forever" possible. We also need priesthood power. Heavenly Father has given to modern-day prophets keys and authority to bind on earth things that will be bound throughout eternity. Temple ordinances are performed by that authority. Jesus referred to the sealing power of the priesthood when he taught his apostles, "Whatsoever thou shalt bind on earth shall be bound in heaven" (Matthew 16:19).

This same power to bind on earth and in heaven was

restored on April 3, 1836, by the ancient prophet Elijah, who appeared to Joseph Smith and Oliver Cowdery in the Kirtland Temple (D&C 110:14–16). Since then, the president of The Church of Jesus Christ of Latter-day Saints has been the keeper of that sealing power. Today, as temple workers are called, some are given this authority to perform marriages for eternity in the temple. Those who are called as temple sealers are set apart by direct authority held by the president of the Church.

Most ordinances in the Church can be performed any-where with the proper authority, but some are so sacred that they are performed only in temples. Because of the sacred nature of temple weddings, the wording of the ceremony is not discussed outside the temple. Suffice it to say that the cer-emony contains the most glorious promises to which we can aspire. I encourage you to read section 132 of the Doctrine and Covenants to gain an understanding of the vital impor-tance of eternal marriage. The sealing ordinance is a crown-ing blessing that you may obtain only in the holy temple.

When my future wife and I had been dating for a couple of months, I went on a trip with her and her parents to the

Las Vegas Nevada Temple. As we gathered in the celestial room, a member of the temple presidency approached us and asked if we would be interested in taking a tour of the temple. We were delighted and followed him with great interest. Our first stop was in one of the temple's sealing rooms. As we observed the beauty of the room, he taught us something special that I will never forget.

"The room we are in is very symbolic," he said. He pointed out the mirrors on the opposing walls and asked us to look at our reflections, which duplicated themselves and seemed to go on forever. He told us that what we were seeing was symbolic of eternal life—the images in one direction pointing to our premortal existence and those in the other direction pointing to our future existence.

He went on to explain that the room we were standing in represented our mortal existence. "Notice how small this room is in comparison with the eternities. This room, situated between the premortal existence and the eternities, represents our second estate, the short time we have on this earth. I want you always to remember that every decision you make while here on earth will have a direct impact on where you will be throughout the eternities."

Understanding that the decisions we make in this life have eternal consequences should motivate us to strive for a temple marriage. The purpose of a temple marriage and the aim of the gospel are to keep us together *and* to make us eligible for Heavenly Father's highest reward—exaltation in the celestial kingdom.

"The most important things that any member of The Church of Jesus Christ of Latter-day Saints ever does in this world are: 1. To marry the right person, in the right place, by the right authority; and 2. To keep the covenant made in connection with this holy and perfect order of matrimony—thus assuring the obedient persons of an inheritance of exaltation in the celestial kingdom."[1]

The Lord has told us that unless we enter into celestial marriage, we cannot reach the highest degree of glory in the celestial kingdom. Eternal life cannot be had in any other way. "In the celestial glory there are three heavens or degrees; and in order to obtain the highest, a man must enter into this order of the priesthood [meaning the new and everlasting covenant of marriage]; and if he does not, he cannot obtain it" (D&C 131:1–3).

This truth is visually demonstrated in the Portland Oregon Temple celestial room, which has three levels. After ascending to the third and highest level, you enter a hallway where the sealing rooms are located. This symbolic floor plan represents the three degrees of glory within the celestial kingdom and the importance of celestial marriage in order to obtain the highest level.

You can easily understand the importance of exaltation in

the celestial kingdom when you realize that only there can you continue to enjoy family relationships established here on earth. When you covenant at the temple altar to be true to your spouse and your Heavenly Father, your marriage will survive death and bind your children to you in an eternal joyous union that will last forever.

President Ezra Taft Benson taught that "God intended the family to be eternal. With all my soul, I testify to the truth of that declaration. May He bless us to strengthen our homes and the lives of each family member so that in due time we can report to our Heavenly Father in His celestial home that we are all there—father, mother, sister, brother, all who hold each other dear. Each chair is filled. We are all back home."[2]

The importance of temple blessings is perhaps most meaningful when death takes a loved one. While I was writing this book, two of my closest friends passed away unexpectedly. We

Portland
OREGON

had grown up together and supported one another while serving missions. Steve and Jason each left behind a wife who was expecting a baby. Attending their funerals was difficult yet inspiring because of the strength demonstrated by their sweet wives and families. Those who loved them the most found peace and understanding, knowing that their painful separation, though likely to last for many years, would be followed by a glorious reunion. Both couples had been married in the temple, thus preventing death from severing their family relationships. During challenging times, the belief that families can be eternal becomes much more than a hope or a wish; it becomes confirmed truth.

Jason's wife, Angie, demonstrated her strength and faith as she shared at Jason's funeral service a letter she had just written to him:

"Dear Jase, I never thought I would be standing here today under these circumstances. All I can say is how grateful I am for the gospel and for our eternal marriage. . . . You are the best and I never could have asked for more. I miss you so much and I look forward to the day when we will be together again. . . . You are truly my one and only. You will always have my heart."

Angie then concluded with her testimony: "I know that my Heavenly Father loves me and will comfort me. I know this gospel is true and that we can be with our loved ones again. I am so grateful that even though Jase had to go, and there is so much that we hadn't done, that we will be a family again. . . . I thank Heavenly Father for the time that he gave me Jason and I am giving him back to Him. I know that we will be together forever again someday."[3] The blessings of the temple are real and will comfort those who partake of them.

Stressing the importance of temple marriage, President Brigham Young said, "There is not a young man in our community who would not be willing to travel from here to England to be married right, if he understood things as they are; there is not a young woman in our community, who loves the Gospel and wishes its blessings, that would be married in any other way; they would live unmarried until they could be married as they should be, if they lived until they were as old as Sarah before she had Isaac born to her. . . . I wish we all understood this in the light that heaven understands it."[4]

Determination to have a temple marriage is illustrated in the story of Kovana Pauga and Evelini Wesley, who lived in Samoa before a temple was built there. To enjoy the blessings of a temple marriage, these two returned missionaries decided to be married in the Laie Hawaii Temple. To cover the cost of airfare to Hawaii, they asked the superintendent of the Church's Vaiola School, where they worked, to withhold 80 percent of their income and set it aside. They paid their tithing with half of their remaining income and lived on the other half. To save money, the couple grew food in a garden. After nearly a year, they had saved enough money to make the trip to Hawaii, where they were sealed for time and eternity in the house of the Lord.[5]

This faithful couple reached their goal because being sealed in the temple was their top priority. Accomplishing things in this life is all about priorities. Pause for a moment and ask yourself how high a priority being married in the temple is for you. Do your actions reflect your desire to be sealed in the temple?

President Heber J. Grant counseled Church members, "I believe that if a person has a desire to do temple work he can

96

find a way to do it. The important thing is the desire. . . . If you get it into your heart and soul that this is one of the most important things you as Latter-day Saints can do, you will find a way to do it."[6] Decide today that being married in the temple is one of the most important things you will do, and the Lord will help you do it!

The first opportunity many Tongan Saints had to partake of temple blessings became available following the dedication of the New Zealand temple in 1958. Thereafter, faithful Tongan Saints began organizing annual excursions to attend the temple in New Zealand. Many members gave all they owned in order to enjoy the blessings of the house of the Lord. Brother Viliami Kongaika and his wife, Lu'isa, desired to be part of the first Tongan group to travel to the temple, but they did not have enough money for their entire family to go to be sealed. Therefore they waited another year while they saved enough money to pay the passage for all family members.

To cover the cost of travel, the Kongaika family sold nearly everything they owned, including their frame house, roofing tin, stove, Viliami's bicycle (their only means of transportation), Lu'isa's sewing machine, and the family's cows, horses, and pigs. The money garnered from these sales allowed the family to travel to the temple the following year, where they were sealed together. Afterward, the Kongaikas returned to face the reality of being without a home, job, or food. Soon after their return, a devastating hurricane destroyed almost everything on the island of Ha'pai, including the Kongaikas' newly built hut. Yet the family recognized the Lord's hand in their lives.

"It was the Lord prompting me to get rid of my goods for a holy cause, because he was going to take them away from me anyway in the hurricane," Viliami said. "I came back from the temple a poor man in terms of worldly goods. But after the hurricane, everyone else was just as poor as we were. The difference between us and them was that we were sealed as an eternal family in the Holy Temple of God."[7]

At the dedication of the New Zealand Temple, President Gordon B. Hinckley attended a testimony meeting of some of the Saints who had traveled from Australia. Describing the meeting, President Hinckley recorded, "A man from Perth, on the far side of Australia, bore his testimony and said, 'We didn't have the means to get here. We lived in Perth. We had to cross all of Australia, almost as far as it is from San Francisco to New York, and then cross the Tasman Sea and come to New Zealand. We couldn't afford it. We had nothing but a little furniture and some dishes and an automobile. We rented the little home in which we lived.'"

President Hinckley said the man related that one evening, while looking across the dinner table at his precious wife and children, he said to himself, "You cannot afford not to go. You can sell your dishes. You can sell your furniture. You can sell your car. Somehow the Lord will help you replace them. But if you should ever fail in your opportunity to bind to you these, your beloved companion and children, you would be poor indeed through all eternity." As a result, he said, "We sold our furniture. We sold our dishes. We sold our car. We sold everything we had and came here. If the Lord will bless me with strength, somehow I will make it up."[8]

The greatest love and happiness available to God's children is found in an eternal family. The gospel of Jesus Christ provides that if we remain true to our temple covenants, we can become exalted families. I have sweet memories of singing

Primary songs about families being together forever and have always had a testimony of this doctrine, but when I held our newborn son, Jacob, for the first time, the possibility of having an eternal family took on a new meaning for me. I was suddenly so grateful to be able to look into his face and know that he was sealed to my wife and me.

Reflecting on that precious moment helps me to more fully understand President Hinckley's words that the temple "speaks of the importance of the individual as a child of God. It speaks of the importance of the family as a creation of the Almighty. It speaks of the eternity of the marriage relationship. It speaks of going on to greater glory."[9] I cherish being able to frequently return to the temple with my wife. Within its walls I am reminded that I possess all I need to be truly happy—forever.

CHOOSING AN ETERNAL COMPANION

Teenage years are wonderful years in which to pursue an education, discover and develop talents, and prepare for a mission and marriage. As you stay close to the Lord and his teachings, the Holy Spirit will guide you in the decisions you make in life, including whom to marry.

President Gordon B. Hinckley said, "Every normal young man desires a wife. Every normal young woman desires a husband. Be worthy of the mate you choose. . . . This will be the most important decision of your life, the individual whom you marry.

"There is no substitute for marrying in the temple. It is the only place under the heavens where marriage can be solemnized for eternity. Don't cheat yourself. Don't cheat your companion. Don't shortchange your lives. Marry the right person in the right place at the right time."[10]

Marrying the right person is vital because marriage is the most intimate and important commitment you will make in life. Your immediate happiness and your eternal joy depend on it. Whether your marriage takes place in the near future or in the distant future, now is the time to prepare. Planning for a temple marriage is the best way to prepare for a successful, loving marriage.

Be certain through prayer and fasting that the person you choose for life and eternity is the right one. Regardless of how attractive, talented, rich, or spiritual someone is, you should not marry that person until both of you have received confirmation from our loving Heavenly Father. He wants us to have joy, and he knows what is best for us.

The person you marry in the temple should be committed

to the Lord and to keeping his commandments. Giving advice on how to choose a companion, President Hinckley said, "Choose a companion you can always honor, you can always respect, one who will complement you in your own life, one to whom you can give your entire heart, your entire love, your entire allegiance, your entire loyalty."[11]

It takes more than a marriage ceremony in the temple for a marriage to be eternal. Lasting marriage requires continued commitment to honoring your spouse and your temple covenants. The marriage seal may be broken if the marriage partners do not remain worthy.

Solidifying your determination to achieve a temple marriage now will help you in choosing whom you should date. Because dating is a preparation for marriage, date only those who have high standards, who respect your values, and who will encourage you to do what you know is right. Marrying the right person results from dating the right people. President Spencer W. Kimball warned, "Do not take the chance of dating nonmembers, or members who are untrained and faithless. A girl may say, 'Oh, I do not intend to marry this person. It is just a "fun" date.' But one cannot afford to take a chance on falling in love with someone who may never accept the gospel."[12] Dating and then marrying someone in the hope that the person will later embrace the gospel is too risky given the significance of marriage. Don't take that chance.

At the age of fourteen, Tamara Bailey made the firm decision to be married in the temple. This was a challenging decision because at the time her family seldom attended church. Making the temple her goal gave her strength to attend seminary and church and to be selective about her friends. When Tamara turned sixteen, a Sunday School teacher counseled, "You will marry someone you date. Make sure you date the kind of person you can marry in the temple."

Following this advice, she asked herself about each person she dated, "Is this the kind of person I could go to the temple with?" When her wedding day arrived, her parents accompanied her to the temple but could not go inside. Of the experience she explained, "They were both with me the day I walked to the doors of the temple. I had finally reached the day when I would enter the temple and receive the blessings I had learned about. The angel Moroni, glowing in the early morning sun on the temple spire, seemed to proclaim my joy to the world. I kissed my parents good-bye as I entered.

"If I had waited to decide where to marry, it would have been too difficult to leave my parents outside and be married inside the temple. I wouldn't have had a strong enough testimony of the gospel and the importance of the temple. I may not even have had the opportunity to decide. Leaders, bishops, and friends helped me. My family supported me. But I never would have made it if I hadn't first *decided* that I was going to the temple.

"In the temple I learned more about Heavenly Father's plan for me. I hadn't reached the end of my goal at all. I had only made one more step. So I *decided* right then to keep my temple promises, no matter how difficult. I *decided* I was someday going to return to my Heavenly Father."[13]

Worthily kneeling at the altar in the house of the Lord, knowing that you and your chosen companion have saved yourselves for each other, will bring you great joy. At the altar you invite the Lord into your marriage, making it a marriage of three, not just of two. Do not settle for anything less.

Live for the day when you will walk hand in hand with

your eternal companion into the beautiful and sacred sealing room of the temple. A sweet spirit of love will fill the room, which will glisten with light. Dressed in white, you and your loved one will gaze into the reflecting mirrors and begin to understand what it means to be sealed for eternity.

As you kneel across the altar from your sweetheart and take each other by the hand, you will experience the loving assurance that you are being married the way the Lord intended. With power and authority, the temple sealer will seal you and your companion for time and all eternity. He will speak inspiring words of counsel and promise you eternal blessings you will hardly comprehend. Afterward, as you leave the temple, you will carry with you in your heart the peace that comes only from being sealed as an eternal family.

Prepare yourself now to be worthy to make the temple an integral part of your life—not just a place to be married but also a place to return to often.

NOTES

1. McConkie, *Mormon Doctrine*, 118.
2. Benson, *The Teachings of Ezra Taft Benson*, 493.
3. Used by permission of the family.
4. Young, *Discourses of Brigham Young*, 195–96.
5. "Eternal Riches," *Church News*, 20 January 1996, 16.
6. Heber J. Grant, "On Going to the Temple," *Improvement Era*, August 1941, 459.
7. Shumway, *Tongan Saints: Legacy of Faith*, 143–44.
8. Hinckley, *Teachings of Gordon B. Hinckley*, 493–94.
9. *Deseret News 1999–2000 Church Almanac*, 480.
10. Gordon B. Hinckley, "Life's Obligations," *Ensign*, February 1999, 2.
11. Hinckley, "Life's Obligations," 2.
12. Kimball, *The Miracle of Forgiveness*, 241–42.
13. Tamara Leatham Bailey, "The Temple-Going Type," *New Era*, April 1998, 35–36.

1
TEMPLE QUESTIONS AND ANSWERS

Here are some questions young people often ask about what they can expect when they go to the temple.

What should I wear when going to the temple?

Proper grooming and clean attire show your respect and preparation for attending the temple. You should dress as you would to attend sacrament meeting. Your grooming and attire should not attract attention or reflect the extreme fads of popular culture. President Packer has given us these thoughtful reminders: "When you have the opportunity to go to the temple to participate in the temple ceremonies or to witness a sealing, remember where you are. You are a guest in the house of the Lord. You should groom yourself and clothe yourself in such a way that you would feel comfortable should your Host appear."[1]

Is it appropriate to try on or wear garments before being endowed?

No. Those going to the temple to be endowed are to carry their garments with them but should not try them on or wear them until instructed to do so in the temple. Garments are available in standard sizes and may be purchased at Beehive Clothing distribution centers.

When I attend the temple for the first time, will anyone be there to help me?

Yes. You don't need to be afraid of being confused or

embarrassed. Help is available every step of the way. While serving as an assistant to the Council of the Twelve and as temple coordinator for the Church, Elder ElRay L. Christiansen said, "One should also know that when you go to the temple for the first time, you will not be left unattended. Temple officiators, receptionists, and others assigned to labor therein will assist you to make your temple experience a beautiful and meaningful one."[2]

What is the significance of wearing white in the temple, and where will I change clothes?

All who attend the temple dress in white, which reminds us that God desires "a pure people" (D&C 100:16). All who serve in the temple are equal in the eyes of our Creator.

"Upon entering the temple you exchange your street clothing for the white clothing of the temple. This change of clothing takes place in the locker room, where each individual is provided with a locker and a dressing space that is completely private. In the temple the ideal of modesty is carefully maintained. As you put your clothing in the locker you leave your cares and concerns and distractions there with them. You step out of this private little dressing area dressed in white and you feel a oneness and a sense of equality, for all around you are similarly dressed."[3]

What covenants do we make in the temple?

Elder James E. Talmage explained that temple covenants include the "promise to observe the law of strict virtue and chastity; to be charitable, benevolent, tolerant and pure; to devote both talent and material means to the spread of truth and the uplifting of the race; to maintain devotion to the cause of truth; and to seek in every way to contribute to the great preparation that the earth may be made ready to receive her King—the Lord Jesus Christ. With the taking of each covenant and the assuming of each obligation a promised blessing is pronounced, contingent upon the faithful observance of the conditions."[4]

Can temple attendance help me make important decisions?

The temple is a peaceful place of refuge from the busyness of the world. It is the house of the Lord, and his Spirit is there. President Ezra Taft Benson said, "In the peace of [our] lovely temples, sometimes we find solutions to the serious problems of life. Under the influence of the Spirit, sometimes pure knowledge flows to us there. Temples are places of personal revelation. When I have been weighed down by a problem or a difficulty, I have gone to the House of the Lord with a prayer in my heart for answers. These answers have come in clear and unmistakable ways."[5]

Why does the Church spend so much money on temples?

At a press conference held during the dedication of the Washington D.C. Temple in 1974, a reporter asked President Spencer W. Kimball how much the temple had cost. President Kimball answered him.

"The reporter then asked, 'Aren't you ashamed of yourself? The money that you have spent on this building would have gone so far in feeding the poor and those who are hungry and in distress in parts of the world.' President Kimball then motioned for Elder Gordon B. Hinckley to respond. He did so by saying, 'We feed the poor. We take care of the needy. We reach out across the world to those in distress. We look after our own. We are doing the work of the Lord. This is a house of God, and nothing is too good for our Father in Heaven.' "[6]

Elder Hinckley further explained, "We have been criticized for the cost of [temples], a cost which results from the exceptional quality of the workmanship and the materials that go into them. Those who criticize do not understand that these houses are dedicated as the abode of Deity and, as Brigham Young stated, are to stand through the Millennium."[7]

Why is a temple marriage so important?

Though the Church recognizes civil marriage as lawful and valid, a civil union binds a couple only for the duration of mortality. Temple marriage binds a couple for eternity. Commenting on the difference between a civil marriage and a temple marriage, President Joseph Fielding Smith said: "Unless young people who marry outside the temple speedily repent, they cut themselves off from exaltation in the celestial kingdom of God. If they should prove themselves worthy, not withstanding that great error, to enter into the celestial kingdom, they go in that kingdom as servants. . . .

"When they marry outside of the temple, they cut themselves off. If they are content with that kind of marriage outside, when they come forth in the resurrection, they have no claim upon each other, or their children upon them, and there will be weeping, wailing and gnashing of teeth."[8]

Do we need an appointment to be married in the temple?

Yes. You should telephone the temple as far ahead of your marriage date as possible to make an appointment. Those who take your phone call will give you detailed instructions about what to bring to the temple, how many guests can be accommodated, who will perform your marriage ceremony, and so forth.

How long is the temple marriage ceremony?

Couples generally spend less than thirty minutes in the sealing room, though the actual ceremony is much shorter.

"The actual temple marriage ceremony lasts less than five minutes. . . . Prior to performing the marriage ceremony the sealer will talk to the couple, giving them solid advice and counsel about their marriage and their new life together. . . . Every sealer draws on his own experience to make these few minutes a very personal prelude to the sealing ordinance. These are very tender moments for the bride, groom, and everyone present."[9]

Does it cost any money to be married in the temple?

No. However, everything of value has a price. The price of admission to the temple is personal worthiness to hold a temple recommend. Couples preparing for temple marriage pay the price of faithful obedience and in return receive the gift of eternal life—"the greatest of all the gifts of God" (D&C 14:7).

What time of day are temple marriages performed?

This depends on the schedule established by each temple. Usually, a marriage can be scheduled whenever the temple is open and a sealing room is available.

What ordinances besides marriage are performed in the temple?

In addition to marriage, temple ordinances include baptism, confirmation, ordination, washing, anointing, endowment, and sealing. These ordinances of exaltation are performed in temples for the dead, while the ordinances of washing, anointing, endowment, sealing, and marriage are also available for the living. We must obtain all of these ordinances before we can enter into the highest of three degrees within the celestial kingdom (D&C 131:1–4).

President Howard W. Hunter taught, "The temple ordinances are absolutely crucial; we cannot return to God's presence without them. I encourage everyone to worthily attend the temple or to work toward the day when you can enter that holy house to receive your ordinances and covenants."[10]

Why are temple baptismal fonts situated below the surface of the earth?

Baptism is an essential ordinance and is symbolic of death, burial, and resurrection. In keeping with that symbolism, the font, which represents the grave, is located underground. The Prophet Joseph Smith wrote, "The baptismal font was instituted as a similitude of the grave, and was commanded to be in a place underneath where the living are wont to assemble, to show forth the living and the dead, and that all things may have their likeness" (D&C 128:13).

What does the baptismal font symbolize?

"The baptismal fonts in the temples of The Church of Jesus Christ of Latter-day Saints are beautiful and yet unique and singular in design," said temple architect Emil B. Fetzer. "They take their basic pattern from the historical and ancient design of the so-called 'sea' of the great temple built by Solomon in Jerusalem as described in the Bible. . . .

"The 'sea' or brazen laver of the great temple built by Solomon is accounted for in some detail in the Bible. (See 1 Kings 7:23–26.) In essence this record states that the "molten sea" was 15 feet in diameter, in the shape of a hemisphere—therefore 7½ feet deep and 45 feet in circumference. Under the brim on the outside were two rows of ornaments cast on the surface. The bowl was placed upon 12 oxen cast of metal. (Undoubtedly these represented the 12 tribes.) Three oxen faced to the north, three to the west, three to the south, and three to the east, and their hind parts were inward, under and supporting the bowl."[11]

How many temples will the Church build?

While discussing the Salt Lake Temple, President Brigham Young said, "This is not the only temple we shall build; there will be hundreds of them built and dedicated to the Lord. This temple will be known as the first temple built in the mountains by the Latter-day Saints. And when the Millennium is over, and all the sons and daughters of Adam and Eve, down to the last of their posterity, who come within the reach of the clemency of the Gospel, have been redeemed in hundreds of temples through the administration of their children as proxies for them, I want that temple still to stand as a proud monument of the faith . . . of the Saints of God in the mountains, in the nineteenth century."[12]

Why do statues representing the angel Moroni adorn most latter-day temples?

These statues have come to symbolize the restoration of the gospel in the latter days. Of the first one hundred temples, only fifteen do not have a statue of the angel Moroni, who is depicted as proclaiming the gospel "to every nation, and kindred, and tongue, and people" (Revelation 14:6).

Why isn't the temple open to everyone?

The temple is open to everyone who joins the Church and is worthy and prepared to enter. Church leaders urge all Latter-day Saints to prepare for their temple blessings, but the

Lord has set restrictions and conditions that his sons and daughters must meet before they can enter his holy house. President Packer said, "The restriction preventing non-members from visiting the dedicated temples does not suggest that there is anything about the building or its appointments that they should not see."[13]

Before a temple's dedication, sufficient time is allotted for a temple open house, which the Church advertises extensively. Anyone interested can tour the temple during an open house and see most temple rooms, but ordinance work within those rooms is not open to the public. Elder ElRay L. Christiansen said, "The ordinances of the temple are so sacred that they are not open to the view of the public. They are available only to those who qualify through righteous living. They are performed in places dedicated especially for this purpose. Their sacred nature is such that discussion in detail outside the temple is inappropriate."[14]

What is the difference between a temple and a meetinghouse?

President Packer clarified the difference: "In the Church we build other buildings of many kinds. In them we worship, we teach, we find recreation, we organize. We can organize stakes and wards and missions and quorums and Relief Societies in these buildings or even in rented halls. But, when we organize families according to the order that the Lord has revealed, we organize them in the temples."[15]

If a man and a woman marry civilly and then later join the Church, can they obtain the blessings of an eternal family?

Couples who have been married civilly may be sealed to one another and to their born and unborn children in a brief and sacred ordinance that is performed in a temple sealing

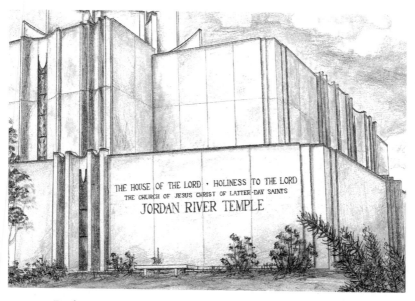

THE HOUSE OF THE LORD · HOLINESS TO THE LORD
THE CHURCH OF JESUS CHRIST OF LATTER-DAY SAINTS
JORDAN RIVER TEMPLE

room. Bishops assist in preparing new converts to attend the temple.

Why do many temples have symbols on their exterior?

Gospel symbols serve as teaching devices. The symbols found on the exterior of the temples reinforce the spiritual teachings revealed in temple ordinances. President George A. Smith wrote, "Every one conveys a moral lesson, and all point to the celestial world."[16] These symbols are visual reminders of the grandeur of God and suggest the order that characterizes his creations. The temple itself is a symbol of God's greatness and of our dependence on the Lord for both our salvation and our life.

What are some of the blessings in this life that come to someone who attends the temple regularly?

Speaking of the blessings that come from attending the temple, President Ezra Taft Benson said: "When you attend the temple and perform the ordinances that pertain to the house of the Lord, certain blessings will come to you: You will receive the spirit of Elijah, which will turn your hearts to your spouse, to your children, and to your forebears. You will love your family with a deeper love than you have loved before. You will be endowed with power from on high as the Lord has promised. You will receive the key of the knowledge of God (see D&C 84:19). You will learn how you can be like Him. Even the power of godliness will be manifest to you (see D&C 84:20)."[17]

The temple is a place to go when you face crucial decisions or carry heavy burdens. Consider these perspectives from former temple presidents:

- "You can't help but leave the temple feeling uplifted. You learn charity and love and compassion. You leave the cares of the day outside the doors of the temple, and when you go out, your feet are led to the paths you've been searching for to help you with some problem you might have.

- "After you make covenants, you're not pulled to and fro by the world so easily. It's a strength to your life and helps you to keep righteous goals."

- "You get a perspective of your life that puts it in order for you. And the experience in the temple is supportive of the LDS way of life. It gives you a backup, a reassurance that what you're doing is righteous."

- "The endowment brings all generations together, no matter what songs your parents or grandparents sang or how they wore their hair. You have that great common bond of the temple."[18]

THE HOUSE OF THE LORD • HOLINESS
THE CHURCH OF JESUS CHRIST OF LATT
JORDAN RIVER TEM

What is the central teaching of the temple?

Engraved on the exterior of the temple are the words, "The House of the Lord," meaning the Lord Jesus Christ. The temple is a holy sanctuary where the Lord may come. All that we do in the temple reminds us of the Savior—his greatness, redeeming sacrifice, and love for us—and qualifies us to return to his presence. The temple ceremony was given by a wise Heavenly Father to help us become more Christlike. By attending the temple we develop the Savior's attributes and renew the covenants we have made to live his teachings.

By performing temple ordinances, we demonstrate our faith and commitment to the Lord and to his Church. The basis of every temple ordinance and covenant is the atonement of Jesus Christ. President Howard W. Hunter taught, "As we attend the temple, we learn more richly and deeply the purpose of life and the significance of the atoning sacrifice of the Lord Jesus Christ. Let us make the temple, with temple worship and temple covenants and temple marriage, our ultimate earthly goal and the supreme mortal experience."[19]

NOTES

1. Packer, *The Holy Temple*, 74.
2. ElRay L. Christiansen, "Some Things You Need to Know About the Temple," *New Era*, June 1971, 27.
3. Packer, 71.
4. Talmage, *The House of the Lord*, 84.
5. Ezra Taft Benson, "What I Hope You Will Teach Your Children about the Temple," *Ensign*, August 1985, 8.
6. Hinckley, *Teachings of Gordon B. Hinckley*, 641.
7. Hinckley, 628.
8. Smith, *Answers to Gospel Questions*, 4:196–97.
9. Robert L. Backman, "Q&A: How Long Is the Temple Marriage Ceremony?" *New Era*, June 1975, 46.
10. Howard W. Hunter, "Follow the Son of God," *Ensign*, November 1994, 88.
11. Emil B. Fetzer, "Q&A: Could You Tell Me a Little about the History of Our Temple Baptismal Fonts? Why Are Oxen Used to Support the Fonts?" *New Era*, March 1976, 26–27.
12. Young, *Discourses of Brigham Young*, 395.
13. Packer, 33.
14. Christiansen, 27.
15. Packer, 8.
16. James H. Anderson, "The Salt Lake Temple," *Contributor*, April 1893, 275.
17. *The Teachings of Ezra Taft Benson*, 254.
18. Kathleen Lubeck, "Preparing for the Temple Endowment," *New Era*, February 1987, 9.
19. Howard Hunter, "Follow the Son of God," *Ensign*, November 1994, 88.

PART THREE

TESTING YOUR TEMPLE KNOWLEDGE

EXCERPTS FROM TEMPLE DEDICATORY PRAYERS

8

TESTING YOUR TEMPLE KNOWLEDGE

1. Where was the first temple built in this dispensation?
   A. Nauvoo, Illinois
   B. Salt Lake City, Utah
   C. Kirtland, Ohio
   D. Manti, Utah

2. The temple endowment in this dispensation was first given to a select few in what place?
   A. Kirtland Temple
   B. A room above Joseph Smith's store in Nauvoo
   C. Nauvoo Temple
   D. Winter Quarters

3. Which temple was originally dedicated in private services by Wilford Woodruff and later dedicated publicly by Lorenzo Snow?
   A. Salt Lake Temple
   B. St. George Utah Temple
   C. Manti Utah Temple
   D. Logan Utah Temple

4. For many years, the president of the Church signed each temple recommend.
   A. True
   B. False

5. What day was the cornerstone for the Salt Lake Temple laid?
    A. May 15, 1856
    B. April 6, 1856
    C. May 15, 1853
    D. April 6, 1853

6. The Saints held general conference in the nearly completed Nauvoo Temple in October 1845.
    A. True
    B. False

7. In which temple did Lorenzo Snow see the Savior?
    A. Manti Utah Temple
    B. St. George Utah Temple
    C. Logan Utah Temple
    D. Salt Lake Temple

8. In 1877, who was appointed president of the St. George Utah Temple?
    A. Wilford Woodruff
    B. John D. McAllister
    C. Thomas P. Cottam
    D. George Albert Smith

9. Joseph Fielding Smith was once president of the Salt Lake Temple.
    A. True
    B. False

10. In which temple was the complete endowment first performed?
    A. Salt Lake Temple
    B. Kirtland Temple

    C. Nauvoo Temple
    D. St. George Temple

11. What ordinances are performed in temples today?
    A. Baptisms, confirmations, and priesthood ordinations
    B. Washings and anointings
    C. Endowments and sealings
    D. All of the above

12. How many oxen hold up the baptismal fonts in latter-day temples?

13. What do the oxen represent?

14. In which temple were baptisms for the dead performed for the founding fathers of the United States?
    A. Salt Lake Temple
    B. St. George Utah Temple
    C. Nauvoo Temple
    D. Logan Utah Temple

15. Which temple has a cornerstone box in which was placed a beautiful limited edition "production seri-cel of Jiminy Cricket, who symbolizes 'conscience,' from the classic 1940 Disney film *Pinocchio* (donated by Walt Disney & Co.)."[1]
    A. Los Angeles California Temple
    B. Orlando Florida Temple
    C. San Diego California Temple
    D. Portland Oregon Temple

16. Which temple is the tallest?
    A. Los Angeles California Temple
    B. Salt Lake Temple
    C. Washington D.C. Temple
    D. Manti Utah Temple

17. Which latter-day temple was the first to be built in Europe?
    A. Bern Switzerland Temple
    B. London England Temple
    C. Frankfurt Germany Temple
    D. Freiberg Germany Temple

18. Which Utah temple was the first in use?
    A. Salt Lake Temple
    B. Logan Utah Temple
    C. Ogden Utah Temple
    D. St. George Utah Temple

19. What happened to the original Nauvoo Temple?
    A. It was burned
    B. It was hit by a tornado
    C. It was destroyed by flood
    D. Both A and B

20. How many years was the Salt Lake Temple under construction?
    A. 10
    B. 25
    C. 40
    D. 30

21. Baptisms for the dead were performed in which river?
    A. Mississippi
    B. Ohio
    C. Missouri
    D. Susquehanna

22. Which temple was the first to have a baptismal font?
    A. Kirtland Temple

B. Nauvoo Temple

C. St. George Utah Temple

D. Salt Lake Temple

23. What is the website address for the Church's FamilySearch®
internet genealogy service?

24. Which temple was the first to be built out of an already-
existing structure?

A. Monticello Utah Temple

B. Logan Utah Temple

C. Cardston Alberta Temple

D. Vernal Utah Temple

25. Which of the following temples do not have an angel
Moroni statue?

A. Mesa Arizona Temple

B. Laie Hawaii Temple

C. Apia Somoa Temple

D. All of the above

26. The foundation rock of which temple was crushed with a
cannon made in France and originally used by the armies of
Napoleon?

A. Kirtland Temple

B. St. George Utah Temple

C. Salt Lake Temple

D. Frankfurt Germany Temple

27. Which of the following temples do not have spires?

A. Laie Hawaii Temple

B. Cardston Alberta Temple

C. Mesa Arizona Temple

D. All of the above

28. Which temple has the tallest angel Moroni statue?
    A. Jordan River Utah Temple
    B. Salt Lake Temple
    C. Washington D.C.
    D. Hong Kong China Temple

29. Which country other than the United States was the first to have more than one temple?
    A. Mexico
    B. Germany
    C. England
    D. Brazil

30. Only the home can compare with the temple in sacredness.
    A. True
    B. False

31. Which temple was the first to be built in the southern hemisphere?
    A. Sydney Australia Temple
    B. São Paulo Brazil Temple
    C. Santiago Chile Temple
    D. Hamilton New Zealand Temple

32. Which temple is the smallest (in square footage)?
    A. Freiberg Germany Temple
    B. Monticello Utah Temple
    C. Laie Hawaii Temple
    D. Anchorage Alaska Temple

33. Which temple is the largest (in square footage)?
    A. Washington D.C. Temple
    B. Los Angeles California Temple

C. Salt Lake Temple

D. San Diego California Temple

34. Moses had a portable temple that the Israelites used as they traveled in the wilderness.

A. True

B. False

Answer key

1. C
2. B
3. C
4. A
5. D
6. A
7. D
8. A
9. A
10. C
11. D
12. Twelve
13. The twelve tribes of Israel
14. B
15. B
16. C (288 feet)
17. A
18. D
19. D
20. C
21. A
22. B
23. *www.familysearch.org*

24. D
25. D
26. B
27. D
28. A
29. B
30. A
31. D
32. D
33. C
34. A

NOTE

1. Mark Skousen, *Sunshine in the Soul,* 79.

9

EXCERPTS FROM TEMPLE DEDICATORY PRAYERS

As you read the following excerpts from temple dedicatory prayers, notice how often the prophets ask the Lord to bless the youth of the Church. Whether speaking in 1893 or 2000, the Brethren have been mindful of the youth. What a marvelous thing it is to have inspired leaders plead with our Heavenly Father in your behalf. Who knows what protection you have enjoyed and what blessings await you as a result of these fervent prayers, offered on sacred occasions by inspired men of God?

SALT LAKE TEMPLE

Dedicated by President Wilford Woodruff
April 6, 1893

"Now we pray for the youth of Zion—the children of Thy people; endow them richly with the spirit of faith and righteousness and with increasing love for Thee and for Thy law."[1]

LAIE HAWAII TEMPLE

Dedicated by President Heber J. Grant
November 27, 1919

"We especially pray thee, O Father in Heaven, to bless the youth of thy people in Zion and in all the world. Shield and preserve and protect them from the adversary and from wicked and designing men. Keep the youth of thy people, O Father, in the straight and narrow path that leads to thee; preserve them from all the pitfalls and snares that are laid for their feet. O Father, may our children grow up in the nurture and admonition of the gospel of thy Son Jesus Christ. Give unto them a testimony of the divinity of this work as thou hast given it unto us, and preserve them in purity and in the truth."[2]

IDAHO FALLS IDAHO TEMPLE

Dedicated by President George Albert Smith
September 23, 1945

"We pray for the youth everywhere, and all organizations calculated to develop their character and spirituality, and all which Thou hast caused to be established for their blessing and instruction, including the Primary Association, Sunday Schools, Young Men's and Young Women's Mutual Improvement Associations, the Church educational system, including the seminaries and institutes, and all the quorums of the Priesthood that have to do with the teaching and instruction of the youth.

"May Thy Holy Spirit be richly imparted to Thy young sons and daughters, that their faith may be enlarged, that they may walk righteously and circumspectly before Thee. We seek Thy blessings for all those who in any way devote their time in teaching the youth of Zion, that they may exercise great wisdom and judgment. May they be inspired in their guidance of Thy precious little ones to lead them into paths of truth and righteousness, that thereby the youth may lay a foundation upon which to establish righteous character and become useful in developing Thy Church and Kingdom in the earth. . . .

"We thank Thee, O our Father, that Thou didst restore that grand and glorious principle of marriage for eternity, and didst bestow upon Thy servant the power to seal on earth and have it recognized in the heavens. We acknowledge this privilege as one of Thy most marvelous gifts to us. May all the youth of Thy Church come to know of its beauty and of its eternal importance to them, and to take advantage of it when they marry. May they, our Father, on the other hand, realize fully that the glorious opportunity for eternal companionship of husband and wife, and the power of eternal increase, may be forfeited by them if they fail, through negligence or indifference, to conform to Thy requirements, or if having taken advantage thereof, they may still through improper conduct lose their blessings."[3]

PROVO UTAH TEMPLE

Dedicated by President Harold B. Lee
February 9, 1972

"We pray for the youth of Zion, for the young and rising generation, for those who must now prepare themselves to bear up the kingdom in their time and season. Keep them from evil; hedge up the way so they may not fall into sin and be overcome by the world. O Lord, bless the youth of Zion and us their leaders that we may guide and direct them aright.

"We know that Thy kingdom shall roll onward, and that hosts of the young and rising generation shall yet stand forth, in power and great glory, as witnesses of Thy name and teachers of Thy law. Preserve them, O our God; enlighten their minds and pour out upon them Thy Holy Spirit, as they prepare for the great work that shall rest upon them."[4]

TOKYO JAPAN TEMPLE

Dedicated by President Spencer W. Kimball
October 27, 1980

"We especially pray Thee, our Father in Heaven, to bless and bear up the youth of Zion in all the world. Shield and preserve and protect them from the adversary and from the words and works of wicked and designing men. . . . Please bless us that we may be able to stir the youth of Zion with a desire for eternal marriage in Thy holy temple."[5]

SEATTLE WASHINGTON TEMPLE

Dedicated by President Spencer W. Kimball
November 17, 1980

"We remember before thee, our Father, the youth of Zion. Bear them up that they shall not falter in defending truth and right. Help them to be clean and worthy and instill in them a desire for eternal marriage in thy Holy Temple."[6]

SYDNEY AUSTRALIA TEMPLE

Dedicated by President Gordon B. Hinckley
September 20, 1984

"Bless the youth, the young men and the young women. May they grow in virtue and in knowledge and in love for thee. May they go forth from this thy house to declare the glad tidings of the gospel to the people of the earth. Wilt thou speak through them with power into the hearts of those they teach.

"May thy saints here covenant with thee to walk in thy ways and follow after thy pattern. At the time of marriage may they kneel at the altars of this thy house, pledging their love and loyalty before thee, angels and witnesses, and here, under the authority of thine everlasting priesthood, may they be sealed for time and eternity according to thy great plan."[7]

JOHANNESBURG SOUTH AFRICA TEMPLE

Dedicated by President Gordon B. Hinckley
August 24, 1985

"Bless the youth, the young men and the young women, that they may walk in virtue and yearn for truth."[8]

ORLANDO FLORIDA TEMPLE

Dedicated by President Howard W. Hunter
October 9, 1994

"Bless the youth who will be baptized for the dead. May this sacred service instill in their minds a greater understanding of thy divine plan, and a stronger resolution to live worthy of every blessing which eventually may become available to them in this thy holy house.

"May those who come to be sealed in marriage kneel at these sacred altars and resolve within their hearts to be ever true and faithful, that the sacred relationships here solemnized may continue with happiness throughout all eternity."[9]

BOUNTIFUL UTAH TEMPLE

Dedicated by President Howard W. Hunter
January 8, 1995

"In a time of departure from safe moorings, may youth of the noble birthright carry on in the traditions of their parents and grandparents. They are subjected to the sophistries of Satan. Help such youth to stand firm for truth. Open wide to their view the gates of learning, of understanding, of service in thy kingdom. Bless them with a lengthened view of their eternal possibilities."[10]

KONA HAWAII TEMPLE

Dedicated by President Gordon B. Hinckley
January 23, 2000

"We pray that the youth of the Church may have a desire to serve the needs of those beyond the veil of death through vicarious baptisms in their behalf. As they do so, may there grow in their hearts a compelling desire to walk as Thou wouldst have them walk, and not after the ways of the world."[11]

LOUISVILLE KENTUCKY TEMPLE

Dedicated by President Thomas S. Monson
March 19, 2000

"Bless the youth in this temple district that they may keep themselves clean from the filth of the world, and be eligible to enter Thy house, here to stand as proxies in baptism for those beyond the veil of death."[12]

MEDFORD OREGON TEMPLE

Dedicated by President James E. Faust
April 16, 2000

"Bless the youth of the Church, dear Father. Lead them in paths of righteousness and truth. Protect them from the alluring and seductive calls of the adversary. May they grow in faith, with testimony in their hearts concerning Thee and Thy Son. May they come to this Thy house to solemnize the most sacred event of their lives, their marriage to partners of equal worthiness, and may the covenants which they will make in this house be kept inviolate throughout their lives."[13]

RENO NEVADA TEMPLE

Dedicated by President Thomas S. Monson
April 23, 2000

"May the youth who come to be baptized in behalf of those who have passed beyond the veil of death feel of Thy Holy Spirit and never forget the importance of the sacred work which they perform. May it have a beneficent effect upon their lives."[14]

VERACRUZ MEXICO TEMPLE

Dedicated by President Thomas S. Monson
July 8, 2000

"Bless the youth of the land, the young men and the young women, that they may grow up in righteousness before Thee. Bless them with love for the Savior of the world, our Lord and Master, that they may pattern their lives after the pattern of His life. May they come to this, Thy House, to be sealed together as husband and wife, under Thy divine plan. Strengthen their will, and fortify their resolution to live as Thou wouldst have them. May Thy work grow and strengthen in this part of Thy vineyard."[15]

NOTES

1. Lundwall, *Temples of the Most High*, 124.

2. "The Dedicatory Prayer in the Hawaiian Temple," *Improvement Era*, February 1920, 288.

3. "Idaho Falls Temple Dedicatory Prayer," *Church News*, 29 September 1945, 10.

4. "Dedication Prayer of Provo Temple," *Church News*, 12 February 1972, 5.

5. "Dedication Prayer for Temple in Tokyo," *Church News*, 8 November 1980, 12.

6. "Dedicatory Prayer for New Seattle Temple," *Church News*, 22 November 1980, 12.

7. "Sydney Temple Is a Gift to the Lord," *Church News*, 30 September 1984, 10.

8. "Dedicatory Prayer Asks for Peace in South Africa," *Church News*, 1 September 1985, 5.

9. "'We Thank Thee for this Beautiful Structure,'" *Church News*, 15 October 1994, 4.

10. "'Magnificent Edifice' Dedicated to the Lord," *Church News*, 14 January 1995, 4.

11. "'Here to Taste the Sweet Refreshment of the Holy Spirit,'" *Church News*, 29 January 2000, 4.

12. "'Bless the Youth in this Temple District,'" *Church News*, 25 March 2000, 4.

13. "Medford Dedicatory Prayer: 'Carry Forward the Great Work,'" *Church News*, 22 April 2000, 5.

14. "'No Longer Simply a Building,'" *Church News*, 29 April 2000, 10.

15. "'May Thy Work Grow and Strengthen,'" *Church News*, 15 July 2000, 5.

SOURCES

Benson, Ezra Taft. *The Teachings of Ezra Taft Benson*. Salt Lake City: Bookcraft, 1988.

———. *So Shall Ye Reap*. Salt Lake City: Deseret Book, 1960.

Cannon, George C., comp. *Gems of Reminiscence: Seventeenth Book of the Faith-Promoting Series*. Salt Lake City: George C. Lambert, 1915.

Conference Reports of The Church of Jesus Christ of Latter-day Saints. Salt Lake City: The Church of Jesus Christ of Latter-day Saints, 1898–.

Cowan, Richard O. *Temples to Dot the Earth*. Salt Lake City: Bookcraft, 1989.

Deseret News 1999–2000 Church Almanac. Salt Lake City: Deseret News, 1998.

For the Strength of Youth. Salt Lake City: The Church of Jesus Christ of Latter-day Saints, 2001.

Hinckley, Gordon B. *Teachings of Gordon B. Hinckley*. Salt Lake City: Deseret Book, 1997.

Holzapfel, Richard Neitzel. *Every Stone a Sermon*. Salt Lake City: Bookcraft, 1992.

Kimball, Spencer W. *The Miracle of Forgiveness*. Salt Lake City: Bookcraft, 1969.

Lundwall, N. B., comp. *Temples of the Most High*. Salt Lake City: Bookcraft, 1993.

McConkie, Bruce R. *Mormon Doctrine*. 2d ed. Salt Lake City: Bookcraft, 1966.

McKay, David L., and Mildred C. McKay. *For His House*. Salt Lake City: Murray Utah Stake, 1978.

Olsen, Nolan P. *Logan Temple: The First 100 Years*. Providence, Utah: Keith W. Watkins and Sons, 1978.

Packer, Boyd K. *The Holy Temple*. Salt Lake City: Bookcraft, 1980.

Shumway, Eric, ed. and trans. *Tongan Saints: Legacy of Faith*. Laie, Hawaii: Institute for Polynesian Studies, 1991.

Skousen, Mark. *Sunshine in the Soul: One Hundred Years of the Mormon Church in Florida*. Winter Park, Fla.: Skousen Publishing, 1996.

Smith, Joseph. *History of The Church of Jesus Christ of Latter-day Saints*. Edited by B. H. Roberts. 2d ed. 7 vols. Salt Lake City: The Church of Jesus Christ of Latter-day Saints, 1932–51.

Smith, Joseph Fielding. *Doctrines of Salvation*. Compiled by Bruce R. McConkie. 3 vols. Salt Lake City: Bookcraft, 1954–56.

———. *Answers to Gospel Questions*. Compiled by Joseph Fielding Smith Jr. 5 vols. Salt Lake City: Deseret Book, 1957–66.

Talmage, James E. *The House of the Lord*. Salt Lake City: Deseret Book, 1976.

Young, Brigham. *Discourses of Brigham Young*. Selected by John A. Widtsoe. Salt Lake City: Deseret Book, 1979.